INVESTING IN OUR CHILDREN

WHAT WE KNOW AND DON'T KNOW ABOUT THE COSTS
AND BENEFITS OF EARLY CHILDHOOD INTERVENTIONS

Lynn A. Karoly

Peter W. Greenwood

Susan S. Everingham

Jill Houbé

M. Rebecca Kilburn

C. Peter Rydell

Matthew Sanders

James Chiesa

Funded by a grant from
The California Wellness Foundation

RAND

The research described in this report was supported by a grant from The California Wellness Foundation.

ISBN: 0-8330-2530-9

RAND is a nonprofit institution that helps improve policy and decisionmaking through research and analysis. RAND's publications do not necessarily reflect the opinions or policies of its research sponsors.

Published 1998 by RAND
1700 Main Street, P.O. Box 2138, Santa Monica, CA 90407-2138
1333 H St., N.W., Washington, D.C. 20005-4707
RAND URL: http://www.rand.org/
To order RAND documents or to obtain additional information, contact Distribution Services: Telephone: (310) 451-7002; Fax: (310) 451-6915; Internet: order@rand.org

Around the beginning of 1997, RAND was approached by the "I Am Your Child" Early Childhood Public Engagement Campaign to conduct an independent, objective review of the scientific evidence available on early childhood interventions. "Early childhood interventions" were defined as attempts by government agencies or other organizations to improve child health and development, educational attainment, and economic well-being. The aim was to quantify the benefits of these programs to children, their parents, and society at large. Funding for the project was secured from The California Wellness Foundation.

RAND's Criminal Justice Program and Labor and Population Program established an interdisciplinary research team including two economists, a criminologist, two mathematical modelers, and a developmental pediatrician. As the project evolved, it became convenient to separate the benefits being examined into two large categories: benefits to the children and parents participating in the programs, and benefits by way of eventual savings to the government (and therefore society in general) from reduced levels of social-service expenditures on participants following the end of the programs. For ease of reference, the first class is typically called "benefits" in this report and the second class, "savings." Savings are compared with program costs.

This study was one of Peter Rydell's last projects at RAND. Peter, who was largely responsible for Chapter Three, died in October 1997. Peter's clear, rigorous approach to the analysis of societal costs, benefits, and savings was a hallmark of RAND research in multiple areas of public policy concern over a period of almost 30 years. His insight, optimism, and generosity have been an inspiration to us all.

CONTENTS

TABLES

Over the last year or so, there has been a renewed interest in the influence of early childhood—especially the first 3 years of life—on child health and development, educational attainment, and economic well-being. Public attention has been stimulated by television shows and stories in national news magazines, and governors and legislators have been initiating programs to direct budgetary surpluses to services for young children. Much of this activity has been given impetus by research findings that the great majority of physical brain development occurs by the age of three. These findings have been interpreted to suggest that early childhood furnishes a window of opportunity for enriching input and a window of vulnerability to such social stressors as poverty and dysfunctional home environments. The response has been an attempt to promote healthy child development, particularly among disadvantaged children, with home visits by nurses, parent training, preschool, and other programs.

It is unclear what will happen to these programs once the media spotlight moves on and budgets tighten. Perhaps a public clamor over the next hot issue will draw funds away from early childhood programs; perhaps it should. The current period of relative largesse provides the opportunity not only to initiate programs but to undertake the kind of rational evaluation of those programs that will help clarify the choices that must eventually be made. In this report, we assemble the evidence now available on early childhood interventions to try to answer two questions that will be of interest to policymakers who must allocate resources and to the public who provides those resources:

- *Do early interventions targeted at disadvantaged children benefit participating children and their families?* After critically reviewing the literature and discounting claims that are not rigorously demonstrated, we conclude that these programs can provide significant benefits.

- *Might government funds invested early in the lives of some children result in compensating decreases in government expenditures?* Here, we examine the possibility that early interventions may save some children (and their parents) from placing burdens on the state in terms of welfare, criminal justice, and other costs. Again, after updating and refining earlier estimates, we find that, at least for some disadvantaged children and their families, the answer to this question is yes.

We use words like "can" and "might" deliberately. We cannot freely generalize these conclusions to all kinds of targeted early interventions, especially not to large-scale programs, because of various limitations in the evidence collected to date. We pay special attention in our analysis to these limitations, which have important implications for future initiatives. In particular, these limitations suggest that better evaluations of new and continuing intervention efforts would be of great value to future decisionmaking.

WHAT ARE THE BENEFITS?

The term "early intervention" can be broadly applied. It can be used for services generally available to and needed by many children, such as immunizations and child care, and to programs not specifically aimed at children, such as Food Stamps and Medicaid. In this report, we restrict its application to programs targeted to overcome the cognitive, emotional, and resource limitations that may characterize the environments of disadvantaged children during the first several years of life.

Even the term "targeted early intervention" is a broad concept. It covers programs concerned with low-birthweight babies and those concerned with toddlers in low-income families; interventions targeting children as well as those targeting their mothers; services offered in homes and those offered in centers; programs aimed at improving educational achievement and those aimed at improving health; and services as diverse as parent skills training, child health screening, child-abuse recognition, and social-services referral.

This diversity makes it impossible to draw overall generalizations about "targeted early intervention" and limits us to inferences as to what some programs *can* do, depending on the characteristics of the program and the families it serves. Furthermore, given the shortcomings and limitations in the design of many early intervention evaluations and the measures omitted from them, what we don't know about the effects of early childhood intervention may exceed what we know (more on this appears below). Nonetheless, our review supports the proposition that, in some situations, carefully targeted early childhood interventions *can* yield measurable benefits in the short run and that some of those benefits persist long after the program has ended.

We reached that conclusion after examining a set of nine programs in which evaluations had been performed that assessed developmental indicators, educational achievement, economic well-being, and health for program participants and compared them with the same measures for matched controls. In most of the programs, controls were selected by random assignment at program outset. We also sought programs with participant and control groups large enough at program implementation and follow-up to ensure unbiased results, although resource limitations on these programs did not always permit that.

Figure S.1 schematically summarizes the results of our review of the effects of these programs on participating children.[1] The filled squares show which of a number of developmental, educational, economic, and health indicators were measured for each program reviewed. Dark gray indicates a favorable (and statistically significant) result, and black indicates no statistically significant

---

[1] The nine programs are the Early Training Project, Perry Preschool, Chicago Child-Parent Center (CPC), Houston Parent-Child Development Center (PCDC), Syracuse Family Development Research Program (FDRP), Carolina Abecedarian, Project CARE (Carolina Approach to Responsive Education), Infant Health and Development Project (IHDP), and Elmira (New York) Prenatal/Early Infancy Project (PEIP). We also review Project Head Start, but results are not summarized in Figure S.1 because there are multiple evaluations that cannot be readily summarized.

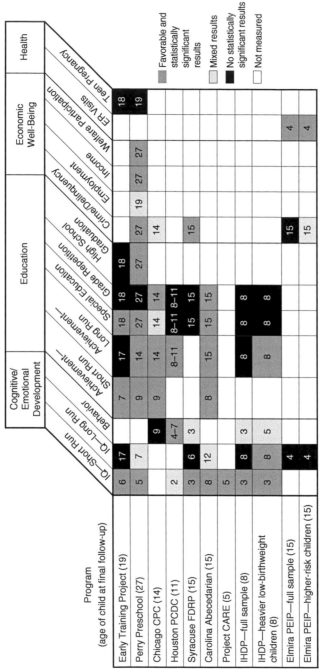

Figure S.1—Effects of Selected Early Intervention Programs on Participating Children

SOURCE: See Table 2.2.

NOTE: Number in box refers to age of child when measure was last taken. When results were mixed (light gray squares), the age refers to the last age when the effect was significant. See text note for full program names.

result; light gray denotes mixed findings.[2] As the figure shows, each program favorably affected at least one indicator, and most of them affected several (that is, participants had better outcomes on these indicators than did children in the control group).[3] Although many studies did not find favorable outcomes across the full range of effects they examined (especially in the long run), favorable effects dominate. A companion analysis of program effects on mothers also showed that measured results tended to be favorable, although the ratio of favorable to null results across all programs was not as high.

The programs thus led variously to the following advantages for program participants relative to those in the control group:

- Gains in emotional or cognitive development for the child, typically in the short run, or improved parent-child relationships.

- Improvements in educational process and outcomes for the child.

- Increased economic self-sufficiency, initially for the parent and later for the child, through greater labor force participation, higher income, and lower welfare usage.

- Reduced levels of criminal activity.

- Improvements in health-related indicators, such as child abuse, maternal reproductive health, and maternal substance abuse.

While many significant differences between participants and controls were found, a statistically significant difference is not necessarily an important one. The size of the difference also needs to be taken into account—and the size of many of the differences could be fairly characterized as substantial. For example, the Early Training Project, Perry Preschool, and the Infant Health and Development

---

[2]A favorable result may be either an increase or decrease in an indicator among program participants relative to controls—depending on the indicator. For example, while a favorable result for IQ means that the IQ was *higher* for treatment children compared with controls, a favorable result for criminal behavior occurs when the incidence is *lower* for the treatment group.

[3]In addition, in most cases even when results were not statistically significant (black in the figure), the difference between treatment and control groups was in the expected direction for the program to produce beneficial results.

Project (IHDP) found IQ differences between treatment participants and controls at the end of program implementation that approached or exceeded 10 points, a large effect by most standards. The difference in rates of special education and grade retention at age 15 in the Abecedarian project participants exceeded 20 percentage points. In the Elmira, New York, Prenatal/Early Infancy Project (PEIP), participating children experienced 33 percent fewer emergency room visits through age 4 than the controls, and their mothers were on welfare 33 percent less of the time. In the Perry Preschool program, children's earnings when they reached age 27 were 60 percent higher among program participants. Thus, we conclude that there is strong evidence to support the proposition that at least some early interventions can benefit participating children and their mothers.

It is also apparent from Figure S.1, however, that for most programs, most indicators are not measured. This is even truer of the maternal analysis, where five of the nine evaluations paid no attention to possible effects on the mother other than parental development. Our analyses thus represent only a partial accounting of program benefits. Furthermore, most evaluations did not involve long-term follow-ups, and some benefits could take a number of years to accrue (some could also erode with the passage of time).

WHAT ARE THE SAVINGS?

Some people may think that the benefits of targeted early intervention programs for participating families are enough to justify public expenditures on them. Others may appreciate the benefits to disadvantaged children but may be reluctant to raise tax burdens to accomplish such goals or may wish, at least, for broader favorable ramifications from an investment of public funds. One source of broader benefit is the potential savings the government (and thus taxpayers) realize when families participating in early interventions require lower public expenditures later in life. Participating children may spend less time in special-education programs. Parents and, as they become adults, children may spend less time on welfare or under the jurisdiction of the criminal justice system. They may also earn more income and thus pay more taxes.

In Figure S.2, we compare program costs with eventual government savings for two of the nine programs—Perry Preschool and the

Elmira PEIP. The Perry Preschool program enrolled 123 disadvantaged African American children in Ypsilanti, Michigan, in the mid-1960s. The program was a part-time preschool that included weekly home visits by the teacher and lasted for one or two school years. For the Elmira PEIP, 400 disadvantaged, primarily nonminority families received home visits by nurses trained in parent education, establishment of support networks for the mother, and linkage of the family to other health and human services. Mothers received an average of 32 visits from the fourth month of pregnancy through the child's second year. We chose these two interventions for three reasons:

- They were random trials that satisfied sample size and attrition criteria.

- They measured progress on developmental, educational, economic, criminal justice, and health measures that could be expressed in monetary terms.

- They followed the children long enough for benefits to accrue. The latest Elmira PEIP follow-up was at age 15 and Perry Preschool at age 27.

For the Elmira PEIP estimates, we followed the approach taken in the evaluation of that project, which was to split the results into two groups. One contained the higher-risk families (those with single mothers *and* low socioeconomic status) and the other the lower-risk families. Costs and savings for the two Elmira PEIP groups and for the Perry Preschool participants are shown in Figure S.2.[4] Costs are known with a fair degree of certainty. The precision of the savings estimates, however, depend on the sample sizes, and the vertical lines indicate the 66 percent confidence band (that is, there is a 66 percent probability that the true benefit level falls along the vertical line). A vertical line of twice the length shown would indicate a 95 percent confidence band.

---

[4]Dollars shown have been converted to present value—i.e., future costs and savings have been discounted (at 4 percent per year) to recognize the standard assumption in economics that, even apart from inflation, people attach less value to future dollars than to current ones. "Present" here is the year of the child's birth. All amounts are in 1996 dollars.

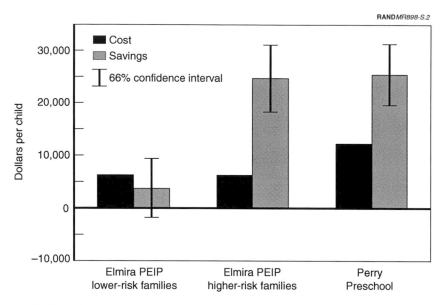

RAND*MR898-S.2*

NOTE: All amounts are in 1996 dollars and are the net present value of amounts over time where future values are discounted to the birth of the participating child, using a 4 percent annual real discount rate.

Figure S.2—Program Cost Versus Savings to Government (Taxpayers)

For the Perry Preschool and the higher-risk families of the Elmira PEIP, our best estimates of the savings to government are much higher than the costs (about $25,000 versus $12,000 for each participating Perry family; $24,000 versus $6,000 for Elmira). Although there is considerable uncertainty with respect to the benefit estimates, from a statistical point of view we can be more than 95 percent certain that the benefits exceed the costs.[5] It is worth pointing out, however, that while benefits exceed costs, the costs accrue immediately, while the benefits are realized only as the years pass and children transition through adolescence to adulthood.

[5]There are however, other uncertainties that are not related to sample size and that cannot be measured with statistical methods.

In the case of the lower-risk participants of the Elmira PEIP, the savings to government are unlikely to exceed the costs. In fact, our best estimate of the net savings is that they are negative: The government savings, while positive, are not enough to offset program costs. This result illustrates the importance of targeting programs to those who will benefit most if the hope is to realize government savings that exceed costs.

We emphasize, however, that while we included the full costs of the programs, we could not account for all benefits. The Elmira PEIP, which has followed participating children only to age 15 so far, provides no basis for calculating the amount these children may save the government in welfare costs, or the extra taxes they may pay as adults. We might expect such savings even for the lower-risk participants, although the longer-run savings may be less than those generated by children in the higher-risk families. The Perry savings may also be underestimated because benefits to mothers were not measured.

Furthermore, the programs generate additional benefits to society beyond the government. These include the tangible costs of the crimes that would eventually have been committed by participating children, had they not participated in the program. The benefits also include the extra income generated by participating families (not just the taxes on that income), which can be reckoned as a benefit to the overall economy. We estimated these two benefit sources combined as roughly $3,000 per family in the case of the lower-risk Elmira participants, about $6,000 per family for the higher-risk Elmira participants, and over $24,000 per family in the Perry case.

While the net savings and other benefits from these programs appear promising, caution must be exercised for various reasons in drawing generalizations for public policy. We explain most of these reasons below, but two relate specifically to the cost-savings approach. First, because these are the only two programs whose evaluation characteristics permit estimates of long-term savings with any accuracy, we cannot say that different programs would also generate such savings (by the same token, we cannot say that they wouldn't). Second, because there was some variation between the two programs in the indicators of success measured, we cannot conclude from the different net savings numbers that one program is better than the other.

One final caveat: Cost-savings analysis is a useful tool because, when the results are positive, it provides strong support for program worth. That is, it shows that only a portion of the benefits—those easily monetizable—outweigh the program's entire cost.[6]   However, because only some of the benefits are taken into account, a negative result does not indicate that a program *shouldn't* be funded. Policymakers must then decide whether the nonmonetizable benefits—e.g., gains in IQ, in parent-child relations, in high-school diplomas—are worth the net monetary cost to the government.

WHAT REMAINS UNKNOWN AND WHAT DOES IT MEAN FOR POLICY?

On the basis of research conducted to date, we know that some targeted early intervention programs have substantial favorable effects on child health and development, educational achievement, and economic well-being. We also know that some of these programs, if targeted to families who will benefit most, have generated savings to the government that exceed the costs of the programs. There is still much that we do not know about these programs, however, and this limits the degree to which these conclusions can be generalized to other early intervention programs. One of the big unknowns is why successful programs work—and others don't. In particular, we do not know the following:

- *Whether there are optimal program designs.* There have not been enough controlled comparisons that can support choices between focusing on parents versus children (or both), intervening in infancy versus the preschool years, integrating interventions versus running them independently, or tailoring to individual needs versus treating children the same but treating a greater number.

- *How early interventions can best be targeted to those who would benefit most.* It is not yet known which eligibility criteria would generate the most positive benefit/cost ratios. In addition,

---

[6]A decision as to whether to fund a program must, of course, also take into account budgetary constraints and other uses for the money.

whatever criteria are used will have dramatic implications for program cost and implementation.

There are other unknowns:

- *Whether the model programs evaluated to date will generate the same benefits and savings when implemented on a large scale.* The demonstrations have been undertaken in a more resource-intensive, focused environment with more highly trained staff than is likely to be achievable in full-scale programs.

- *What the full range of benefits is.* Typically, evaluations have focused on those aspects of development that the intervention was intended to influence. But we know from some studies that programs can have a broad array of effects beyond their principal objectives.

- *What the implications of the changing social safety net are.* Previous demonstrations were carried out under the now-superseded welfare system. To some extent, those interventions depended on that system for collateral support of families, and the savings generated were partly in terms of welfare costs that the government may not now be paying out anyway.

These unknowns will have to be resolved if wise decisions are to be made among early intervention alternatives and if the programs chosen are to be designed to fully realize their potential for promoting child development—and saving money. In particular, research is needed into *why* programs work. Otherwise, inferences cannot be drawn about new program designs, and every such design would be unproven until tested and evaluated.

The scope of further research should depend on the specific information sought or the scale of the program. *New demonstrations are needed* to answer questions that require variations in program design or that reflect the evolving society and economy, and broader testing of previous designs is required to answer questions of scale-up. However, on questions of targeting, benefits beyond objectives, and other issues, much could also be gained—and less expensively—by *making the most of evaluations already under way*—e.g., by further follow-ups and expansion of the set of benefits measured. Finally, where governments see fit to initiate large-scale public programs on the basis of current knowledge, *careful evaluation should be a component*. Then, when budgets tighten again and choices need to be made, the worth (or lack of worth) of these programs will be more firmly established.

The research required represents a substantial commitment of funds—most likely in the millions or even the tens of millions of dollars. However, the early intervention programs that may prove warranted (and that some people are already advocating) will represent a national investment in the hundreds of millions or billions of dollars. A modest if substantial expenditure initiated now could thus ensure that maximum benefits are achieved from a much larger expenditure over the long term.

ACKNOWLEDGMENTS

We thank Rob Reiner and his colleagues at the "I Am Your Child" Early Childhood Public Engagement Campaign for providing the impetus for this study and for helping arrange funding for it. Although Mr. Reiner has been working on behalf of increased public funding for early childhood intervention, he saw the importance of an objective analysis of costs and benefits, and we have been aided by his consultation over the course of the study.

RAND colleagues James Kakalik and David Grissmer reviewed two drafts of this report, and their comprehensive and constructive criticisms sharpened our analysis and informed our presentation. We were also assisted at various points along the study by comments and other information from Phyllis Ellickson and Gail Zellman at RAND; Arleen Leibowitz and Neal Halfon at the University of California, Los Angeles; David Olds at the Prevention Research Center for Family and Child Health, Denver, Colorado; and Steven Barnett at Rutgers University, New Brunswick, New Jersey.

We are also indebted to Jane Ryan for coordinating book design, production, and marketing; Christina Pitcher for editing the manuscript; and Nora Wolverton for production assistance.

Finally, there would have been no study without funding from The California Wellness Foundation, and we are much in debt to Gary Yates, president of the foundation, and his staff. One of the authors (Jill Houbé) also received support from the Robert Wood Johnson Clinical Scholars Program and the Agency for Health Care Policy Research.

Chapter One

INTRODUCTION

Over the last year or so, there has been a renewed interest in the importance of early childhood, especially the first 3 years of life. Public attention has been stimulated by cover stories in national news magazines (Nash, 1997, and a special edition of *Newsweek*, Spring/Summer 1997), a 1997 White House conference on early childhood development, and an ABC television special sponsored by the "I Am Your Child" Early Childhood Public Engagement Campaign. These recent efforts continue earlier initiatives that highlighted the need to understand and enhance early childhood development (see, for example, the Carnegie Corporation of New York, 1994 and 1996).

Politicians and other policymakers, motivated by strong public support for initiatives targeting children, are seeking new ways to direct public sector resources toward the period of earliest child development. This enthusiasm for programs that benefit children is demonstrated by such groups as the National Governor's Association (NGA), which devoted several meetings in 1997 to the subject of early childhood intervention. At these sessions and elsewhere, governors across the range of the political spectrum have been eager to show their support for new early childhood initiatives (NGA, 1997). The recent welfare reform legislation has further prompted politicians and policymakers to look to new models for providing assistance to disadvantaged children and their families.

The growing interest in early childhood comes at a time when fiscal restraints may be lifting so that more resources are available to spend on public programs for children. Strong economic growth has resulted in a steady decrease in the federal budget deficit, and many states now face budget surpluses. With the prospect of surplus funds, federal, state, and local governments are considering new investments in children, particularly during early childhood. New initiatives include developing education and outreach programs for parents, increasing funding for Head Start or other preschool programs, and expanding subsidies for or improving the quality of child care for young children.

With the alignment of public support and relative fiscal largesse, there exists a window of opportunity, unprecedented in recent decades, to implement new public-sector programs focused on young disadvantaged children. To maximize the benefit of any new spending, policymakers and the public should understand what we do—and do not—know about the costs and benefits of early childhood intervention. What is the promise for these investments? What do we know about how to make the most of any new spending on young children?

THE IMPORTANCE OF EARLY CHILDHOOD

The renewed interest in early childhood is stimulated by a growing body of evidence from a diverse array of disciplines that continues to confirm what many have felt must be true: The period of early childhood, from conception through at least age 3, is critical to a child's development. The work of Bowlby, Gesell, Piaget, Watson, and others has provided important insight into the critical events occurring in infancy and early childhood, including mother-infant bonding, emotional regulation, and the basis for language development (Bowlby, 1969; Gesell and Thompson, 1934; Piaget, 1947; Piaget and Inhelder, 1947; Watson, 1913). Research and clinical work have found that the experiences of the infant and young child provide the foundation for long-term physical and mental health as well as cognitive development.

Neurologists have found what may be a biophysical basis for these results. It has been known for some time that the human brain achieves approximately 85 percent of its adult size (as measured by weight) by age 2 1/2 years, and 90 percent of total growth by age 3 (Purves, 1994). This period of brain growth corresponds to the young child's attainment of important developmental milestones, including emotional regulation and attachment, language development, and motor skills (Sander, 1987).

Research in brain science suggests that this increase in brain size does not occur through the addition of new brain cells. Instead, it comes about as a result of changes in cell size and maturity and in the complexity of connections among the brain cells present at birth. Many factors in the environment contribute to this critical shaping of cell connections in infancy and toddlerhood, including physical, socioemotional, cognitive, and nutritional conditions. The number and complexity of connections more than triple by 4 months of age alone (as estimated by protein to DNA ratios of the cells, Cowan, 1979; Epstein, 1979). This measurable growth of intercellular communication represents changes due in part to brain "plasticity"—the capacity of the growing brain to respond to outside influences.

The brain, which reaches its full size in adolescence, continues to be malleable throughout an individual's lifetime although the regions of the brain where synaptic restructuring occurs vary by age (Solso, 1997). In addition to the first 3 years, other periods of brain development and restructuring occur at regular intervals during childhood as environmental influences continue to shape neural connections. Nevertheless, recent research suggests that the early years of brain development provide an important foundation for future emotional and cognitive functioning (Purves, 1994; Schore, 1994).

The period of early childhood development is thus unique—physically, mentally, emotionally, and socially. It is a period of both opportunity and vulnerability. A growing body of literature identifies a number of factors that mediate whether this crucial period of child development is positive or negative, with both biological and environmental stressors potentially compromising a child's healthy development (Barnett, 1995). For example:

- Children with a reduced level of parental stimulation or emotional support may also exhibit socioemotional problems in childhood that are associated with behavior problems later in life (Spitz, 1965; Cohen and Beckwith, 1979; Carlson et al., 1989; Lyons-Ruth, Alpern, and Repacholi, 1993).

- Children may face resource constraints—due to low family income or inadequate nutrition or health care—that limit their development during this period, with consequences for outcomes in adolescence or adulthood (Bradley and Caldwell, 1980; Haggerty, 1984; Parker, Greer, and Zuckerman, 1988; Duncan and Brooks-Gunn, 1997).

At present, we cannot with accuracy identify those children who are at greatest risk. We do know, however, that multiple risk factors place children at even greater disadvantage (Sameroff and Chandler, 1975). And various risk factors and combinations thereof have been used to identify classes of children for whom early intervention with the child or with his or her family may mediate environmental stressors and promote healthy development (Zeanah, 1993). For example, it has been shown that reduction in the incidence of elevated blood lead levels and improved nutrition in children can prevent permanent deleterious effects on development and IQ (Pollitt, 1997; Schwartz, 1994).

WHAT IS EARLY INTERVENTION?

Early childhood interventions are formal attempts by agents outside the family to maintain or improve the quality of life of youngsters, starting with the prenatal period and continuing through entry into school (i.e., kindergarten or first grade). Naturally, much of the support children receive during these early years will come from their families, relatives, and friends. The intent of early intervention is to work with the family to enhance or supplement this support and thus lay the best possible foundation for future health, and for future academic and social functioning.

Early intervention can be broadly understood to include health, education, and social services, and specific interventions may encompass all of these domains, crossing academic disciplines and areas of bureaucratic purview. Examples of early intervention efforts include the following:

- Public health programs that provide prenatal care, immunizations, or nutritional supplements or that seek to prevent injuries.

- Child care programs that regulate the quality of providers in the market or that provide subsidies to families for the purchase of child care or to providers for the provision of services.

- Income or in-kind support programs, including welfare and other social safety-net programs (e.g., the Special Supplemental Feeding Program for Women, Infants, and Children (WIC) and Early and Periodic Screening Diagnosis and Treatment (EPSDT) services).

- Programs intended to promote early childhood development, such as home visitation programs, parenting classes, Early Head Start, Head Start or Healthy Start, preschool and kindergarten, and Part H infant and toddler programs under the Individuals with Disabilities Education Act.

Early intervention can also be interpreted to include programs not focused solely on children, such as Medicaid, Food Stamps, Temporary Assistance for Needy Families (TANF) (formerly Aid to Families with Dependent Children), and Supplemental Security Income (SSI).

As suggested by this array of examples, early childhood programs may serve children directly or they may accomplish their goals through family and parental support, or they may do both. In some cases, the programs and the services they provide benefit all children; examples include those that seek to immunize all children by certain ages, or those that attempt to prevent serious accidents or injuries (e.g., car safety regulations and regulations for toys and other children's products). In other cases, the programs are intentionally targeted to a subset of children. These may be children with disabilities or children exposed to the stressors discussed in the preceding section. These programs may be based on such criteria of need as low income, presence of only one parent, or lagging development. Many programs, especially targeted ones, are designed to compensate for resource deficiencies in early childhood, often brought on by low income and manifesting themselves as poor nutrition or a lack of access to medical care. In some cases, programs are also designed to compensate for one or both of the other risk factors we mentioned—impaired emotional support and reduced cognitive stimulation.

Many early childhood programs, such as Medicaid, WIC, Part H programs, and Head Start, are at least partially subsidized by government funding. In other cases, the government role is accomplished through standards and regulations for goods and services provided to children and their families (e.g., safety or child care standards).

Other services, such as some parent education programs and child care, are provided through private businesses and organizations. Many parents purchase early childhood services themselves.

Many early intervention programs, especially those implemented first on a smaller scale, are accompanied by evaluations to determine whether the programs actually achieve their intended goals. Some evaluations consist of formal experimental or quasi-experimental designs, where children participating in the program are compared with nonparticipating children in terms of their progress along certain developmental measures. Participating and nonparticipating children may or may not be randomly assigned to their respective groups. Comparisons of family support or maternal well-being may also be made. In some cases, these studies follow participating and nonparticipating children long after the intervention to examine outcomes later in childhood or in early adulthood.

Programs to which the term "early intervention" may be applied thus vary greatly in scope, target population, funding, and character of the action undertaken. In this report, we will, for the most part, restrict our use of the term to targeted early intervention programs promoting the development of children subjected to one or more stressors. These targeted early intervention programs primarily include those listed under the fourth bullet above. We are also interested in public policy and will thus focus on programs that are or could be funded by the government.[1]

Even within this narrower area of focus, early intervention programs are proliferating—often without a solid understanding of the costs and benefits they will generate. Currently, over half of the states have one or more new programs under way providing universal or targeted services for infants and toddlers and their families (NGA, 1997). Notable examples include the following:

- Smart Start, a North Carolina program to increase children's access to quality child care, health care, and other critical services.

---

[1] For reviews of the effects of other public programs on child outcomes see Currie (1995). For studies that focus on child care in particular, see Clarke-Stewart (1991), Phillips, McCartney, and Scarr (1987), Studer (1992a, 1992b), and Zaslow (1991).

- Success by Six, a Vermont program that includes a mix of services during early childhood, such as welcome-baby visits for every family and parent support groups.

- Healthy Families Indiana, which promotes healthy child development for children in the state through intensive home visits and parent education classes, among other services.

Such programs can be expected to expand, considering the priority given early childhood development by such governors as Bob Miller of Nevada, former chairman of the NGA, and George Voinovich of Ohio, the new chair of the NGA.

GOALS AND APPROACH OF THIS STUDY

Given the increasing popularity of targeted early intervention programs, the time is opportune for a critical review of such programs and their evaluations. What do the evaluations show? Are they scientifically sound? When we discount those that are not sound, what are we left with? In this study, we address these issues to provide an answer to the overarching question of policy concern: *Do targeted early interventions measurably benefit participating children and their families?*

Some people may think that the benefits of targeted early intervention programs for participating families are enough to justify public expenditures on them. Others may worry about the costs—which may cause an increasing tax burden or cause money to be taken from other beneficial programs. But, from an economic viewpoint, money spent on early intervention may not be uncompensated. Childhood immunizations, for example, have been shown to yield economic as well as health benefits. By some estimates, they save, for each program dollar spent, between $6 and $30 in direct medical costs that would have been incurred had the disease and its complications not been prevented (Centers for Disease Control, 1990; Hay and Daum, 1990; Hinman and Koplan, 1984; White et al., 1985). WIC has been estimated to save between $1.77 and $3.13 in Medicaid costs per program dollar spent (Mathematica, 1990). Other programs may save the government money by keeping children off welfare or out of the criminal justice system. We thus seek to answer a second major policy-relevant question: *Might government funds invested early in the lives of some children result in compensating decreases in government expenditures?*

To address these questions, we draw on an extensive body of literature that has documented the results from an array of targeted early intervention programs.[2] We endeavor to provide an objective assessment of the strength and implications of the evidence on the costs of early childhood interventions and on their potential benefits to children, their parents, and society at large. In our assessment, we present the results of various researchers in a common framework for the benefit of an audience interested in policy. We also employ traditional cost-benefit methodologies to assess, for those programs where the data support such analysis, the savings to government that arise from intervention programs, relative to the costs of those programs.[3] When possible, we also endeavor to take a more comprehensive view by accounting for some of the benefits of such programs to society beyond those accruing to the government. While our assessment of the existing literature points to the tremendous amount of information that we already have about programs and the benefits they produce, there is still much that we have yet to learn. The issues that remain and their relevance for policy are explored as well.

In this report, we are concerned with public policy—with the benefits and costs of interventions that are or could be funded by the government, and with the implications of those benefits and costs for future government action. Much of the debate about the design and implementation of early interventions is centered on the difficulties of deciding what supports are necessary for which children, and who should pay for them. Our findings have some bearing on those issues although this is not a central focus of our analysis. We recognize that, by concentrating on benefits and costs of specific programs, we ignore other important aspects of the debate about early interventions—aspects related to implementation and integration of programs. Issues such as gaps or overlaps in existing program coverage

---

[2]For recent reviews of this literature, see, Meisels and Shonkoff, 1990; Seitz, 1990; Benasich, Brooks-Gunn, and Clewell, 1992; Olds and Kitzman, 1993; Barnett, 1995; Yoshikawa, 1995; Guralnick, 1997; and Reynolds et al., 1997.

[3]For other cost-benefit assessments of early childhood intervention programs, see Barnett (1993); and Olds et al. (1993).

and fragmentation of services currently available to disadvantaged children and their families are beyond the scope of this study.

ORGANIZATION OF THIS REPORT

We begin in the next chapter by discussing the theoretical under-pinnings that motivated researchers to design and test targeted early intervention programs. The types of programs and the deficits they are intended to compensate for are enumerated as a way to illustrate the diverse array of early intervention program models. We show that, despite their diversity, well-designed programs can produce tangible benefits for children and their families in one or more of four broad domains: cognitive development, education, economic self-sufficiency, and health. Many of these benefits are seen long after the intervention has ended, although some do decay as the participants age.

Based on this review, the third chapter presents a cost-savings analysis of two programs reviewed in the second chapter. These two programs included experimental and control groups with initial samples large enough, attrition small enough, and follow-up long enough so that we have reasonable confidence in the estimates of program costs and benefits. Furthermore, the studies measured a set of benefits that can be readily monetized and compared with costs. For these two programs then, we address the question: Do the savings to government exceed program costs? While the bottom-line answer is yes, the analysis reveals that the savings do not always accumulate rapidly, so that the payoff may be years after the intervention has ended. In addition, the savings to government are more likely to exceed costs the more carefully targeted the intervention is.

While the existing literature sheds light on a variety of successful models of early childhood intervention, there are many issues that remain to be addressed, especially as policymakers begin to invest—or at least consider investing—more resources in early childhood intervention programs. The fourth chapter summarizes what we know—and don't know—about early childhood intervention. It presents our assessment of the issues that need to be explored further as researchers and policy analysts continue to study this field, along with the implications of our findings for a wide variety of organizations active in this area. In the end, we believe future investments in children and the programs that serve them must be accompanied by a coordinated, comprehensive research program that will reveal which investments have the greatest payoff. Only in this way can scarce public resources be optimally targeted to the greatest benefit of children and their families.

Chapter Two

TARGETED EARLY INTERVENTION PROGRAMS AND THEIR BENEFITS

In this chapter, we assemble the evidence regarding the benefits of targeted early childhood intervention for program participants. We do this principally by reviewing the evolution of targeted early intervention programs from the initial efforts in the 1960s to the present, highlighting the findings from formal evaluations of several of the most noteworthy programs. We conclude by summarizing the evidence available across programs.

THE ORIGINS OF EARLY INTERVENTION

Early intervention as we know it today is the consequence of over 300 years of social, political, and academic influences. Many of the fundamental theories upon which today's interventions are founded have their origins in early concepts of childhood development.

The earliest modern influences are the writings of European philosophers of the Enlightenment who were among the first to envision childhood as a separate period in life subject to unique developmental influences (Aries, 1962). The debate concerning "nature versus nurture" can be traced to the theories of Locke and others who considered the child a tabula rasa, or clean slate, upon which the environment and upbringing were entirely influential (Meisels and Shonkoff, 1990). This is in contrast to the belief that children are born with genetically predetermined attributes that the environment can do little to change.

This debate continues to echo today through academia and society at large. Many theorists now consider a hybrid of these views to be the most accurate depiction of early childhood potential: While children are born with certain innate capabilities, they are subject to the influences of environment and parenting, and it is a combination of these factors that contributes to later functioning (Carey and Gelman, 1991).

The social construct of childhood evolved in the 19th century into a family-centered model as the industrial revolution created the possibility of a childhood sheltered from adult responsibilities (Aries, 1962). European influences on early childhood theory were prominent at this time, with the emergence of an organized early education curriculum in Germany designed by Friedrich Froebel. These first "kindergarten" classes were designed to promote religious value–based child development through structured play activities (Meisels and Shonkoff, 1990).

Child development theory was also influenced by the evolution of the social sciences and the application of scientific methods of observation, data collection, and analysis to studies of human populations. The scientific approach drew support from the positivist theorists of this period, who believed that there were universal truths about society that once revealed would lead to the resolution of society's problems (Lubeck, 1995). The turn of the century saw the first theories and tests of intelligence developed by Binet and Simon in Paris, and their use to distinguish intellectual capabilities of children (Flanagan, Genshaft and Harrison, 1997). These tests rapidly gained popularity within American culture.

The importation of the kindergarten curriculum to the United States coincided with dramatic changes in the urban American landscape as new waves of immigrants began arriving in American cities. While the middle classes embraced kindergarten as a means to improve child development, the poor urban environment and the growing heterogeneity of the population led social activists to promote the kindergarten curriculum as an important service for immigrants (Ramey, Dorval, and Baker-Ward, 1983). It was hoped that kindergarten would compensate for economic disadvantage in early childhood experiences, promote cultural assimilation, and provide safe child care for working mothers in urban industrial slums (Cohen, 1996).

This call for targeting early intervention to an "at-risk" population is one of the first encroachments upon the Anglo-American tenet of *parens patriae*. This principle considers intervention in a child's upbringing to be justifiable only when parents cannot or will not care for their children (Melton and Megan, 1993). Advocates of early education for immigrants felt that urban conditions were sufficiently deficient to require intervention in the care and upbringing of these children. Early interventionists, under the rubric of "child saving," advocated center-based early education partly to remove children from homes considered economically and culturally impoverished (Swadener and Lubeck, 1995; Zigler, 1990).

Soon after the kindergarten movement made its way to the United States, the "nursery school" curriculum was designed in London by Rachel and Margaret McMillan. In its first incarnation, the nursery school was also a targeted program that began as an urban health clinic (Meisels and Shonkoff, 1990). As it evolved, the nursery school became a comprehensive program designed to improve both education and health. In the United States, the nursery school became a desired "universal," but privately funded, service purchased by middle and upper class families as a means of enabling children to achieve future success (Cohen, 1996).

Continued efforts in the late 19th century to improve urban conditions for children included the opening of "settlement houses" in impoverished communities. Lillian Wald, who founded the Henry Street Settlement in New York City in 1893, and Jane Addams, who established Hull House in Chicago in 1889, were prominent social activists whose work led to a call for federal intervention in the plight of poor children (Hutchins, 1994). This work culminated in the White House Conference of 1909 called by President Theodore Roosevelt, which in turn led to the creation of the federal Children's Bureau in 1912, the first federal agency concerned exclusively with the health and well-being of children (Parmelee, 1994).

The research on infant mortality sponsored by the Children's Bureau led to the Sheppard-Towner Act of 1921, which established maternal and child health services in each state funded through federal grants-in-aid matched by state funds (Hutchins, 1994). This was the first expression of a national child welfare policy establishing the responsibility of states and communities to provide services to improve early childhood. This act was quite controversial and was opposed by the Roman Catholic Church, the U.S. Public Health Service, and the American Medical Association (AMA) (Hutchins, 1994).[1]

Until the 1920s, there was little scientific data on the normal developmental and physical milestones of childhood. The work of Arnold Gesell, a strongly nativist theoretician, established the first parameters of normal and abnormal child development (Gesell and Thompson, 1934). His research provides the foundation for measurement tools used to assess development today. Other movements in child development research included behavioral theorists, such as John B. Watson, who, unlike Gesell, believed that the most important determinants of development were environmental (Watson, 1913). The White House Conference on Child Health and Protection of 1930 was called to draw upon the growing body of research of the 1920s on children's normative growth and development. The Children's Charter—19 statements describing the education, health, welfare, and protection conditions required for optimal child development— was the landmark product of the White House conference.

The 1930 conference paved the way for expansion of maternal child services in the enactment of Title V of the Social Security Act of 1935. This act authorized grants-in-aid to states for expanded child welfare services, and for maternal and child health programs. It recognized the dependence of children on society for their welfare and acknowledged a responsibility for improving social as well as health conditions (Hutchins, 1994).

The federal role in provision of non-health-related child services grew during World War II as large numbers of middle- as well as working-class women entered the workforce. Federally supported child care and nursery schools were created under the Lanham Act during the 1940s to care for children of working women. The emphasis on early education in child care became more prominent

---

[1]It was the AMA's opposition that led a group of physicians belonging to the new profession of pediatrics to establish the American Academy of Pediatrics (AAP) in 1930 (Hutchins, 1994).

with the increase in middle-class use of these services. After the war, however, federal subsidizes for nursery schools virtually disappeared as many of these women left the workforce. Nursery schools in the 1950s once again became the privilege of the middle classes (Meisels and Shonkoff, 1990).

In the post–World War II era, developmental research was strongly influenced by psychoanalytic theory and the examination of deprivation in early childhood. Ainsworth, Bowlby, Anna Freud, and others developed the first theories of mother-child attachment in the 1950s (Ainsworth et al., 1978; Bowlby, 1969; Burlingham and Freud, (1949a, 1949b, 1950). Erikson advanced a theory of normal emotional development (Erikson, 1985). The study of causes of mental retardation became prominent as Piaget's work on normal cognitive development became well known (Piaget, 1947; Piaget and Inhelder, 1947).

Postwar affluence may have contributed to the increasing focus of the lay public on child rearing and development. The popular conceptualization of genetic predetermination of personality and intelligence began to give way under the influence of the academic writings of Donald Hebb, J. McVicker Hunt, and Benjamin Bloom. Hebb's neuropsychological theory examined the dependence of learning later in life on the quality and quantity of early experiences (Hebb, 1949). Hunt emphasized the importance of the first 3 years of life and argued that early environmental influences were the most powerful determinants of child outcomes (Hunt, 1961). Bloom theorized that 50 percent of intellectual development occurred by age 4, implying that a child's development will be most affected by environmental influences in this period of rapid intellectual development (Bloom, 1964). The theoretical groundwork was laid for the debates of the following three decades regarding the causes of abnormal child development and the optimal means of preventing and improving it.

FROM THEORY TO PRACTICE: DETERMINING WHICH INTERVENTIONS WORK

With a twentyfold increase in federal spending on social programs from 1950 to 1979, policymakers and social scientists alike appreciated the need to study how programs were implemented and what results they produced (Shadish, Cook, and Leviton, 1995). Evaluation research has filled the need for a systematic and scientific approach to assessing the conceptualization, design, implementation, and utility of interventions (Rossi and Freeman, 1993).

The difficulty in drawing conclusions about the success of early intervention programs is that the analytic methodology of evaluation has evolved side by side with the programs targeted for study. Our ability to judge the effectiveness of early programs is frequently constrained by the limitations of early outcome measures. For example, early researchers generally assumed that program effects would be specific and immediate, and evaluations were not designed to measure broad or long-term outcomes (Shadish, Cook, and Leviton, 1995).

There are also intrinsic incompatibilities between social science evaluation methods and social service delivery (Weiss, 1972). While properly implemented randomized control trials remain the ideal in terms of evaluation methodology, evaluators must frequently adjust their research methods to the priorities and time constraints of the program they are attempting to study. Experimental-design considerations, such as specific "treatments" and randomized assignment of participants, often do not readily accommodate the service function of intervention programs. Implementing randomized trials and other evaluative methods also takes money away from service provision, and it may be considered unethical to deny control groups access to services. In addition, even with random assignment in longitudinal studies, differential and possibly nonrandom attrition between treatment (or experimental) and control groups may also bias findings from experimental designs, especially when sample sizes are small.

Many of the criticisms directed at early intervention evaluations have to do with the drawing of causal inferences from quasi-experimental and nonexperimental study designs that do not employ random assignment (Reynolds and Temple, 1995).[2] Nonrandom assignment

---

[2]Nonexperimental studies are those in which there is no comparison group. A comparison group is a set of children who are similar to the program participants in as many ways as possible except that they do not participate. The best way to ensure a

may not control for differences in observed and unobserved characteristics between children who participated in an intervention and the comparison group. This may lead to potential bias in estimates of the program's effectiveness and the necessity of cautious interpretation of study results. Because there is often no single or simple way to analyze nonexperimental and quasi-experimental data, controversy surrounds the outcomes claimed for early intervention and will continue to do so (General Accounting Office (GAO), 1997). There are, however, statistical techniques for evaluating quasi-experimental and nonexperimental studies that researchers may use to make estimates of program effects. Newer techniques reduce selection bias by incorporating selection into the analytic model. Reanalysis of previously studied programs has found in some cases favorable effects due to early intervention programs where previously none were recognized (see, for example, Currie and Thomas, 1995, and Reynolds and Temple, 1995).

The political context of social service programs is also an important factor in program and evaluation design, completion, and reporting (Weiss, 1973). Social programs and their evaluations are subject to the ideological debate that gives rise to them, and evaluations that do not support a political view may not find a public venue. Basic political assumptions of service providers may also limit the ability to fully assess the limitations or successes of certain programs.

Finally, most programs have multiple stakeholders who require different questions to be answered by evaluation studies, or who may have little if any interest in measured outcomes (Shadish, Cook, and Leviton, 1995). The literature available on many early intervention programs reflects the diversity of research interests and reinforces the difficulty in drawing common conclusions from different intervention programs and their evaluations.

Together, these issues of study and analysis design raise concerns about the predictive value of the research on early intervention (GAO, 1997). Other issues concern social science research in general.

---

matched comparison group is to recruit a set of children for the program and randomly assign some to the program; the remainder constitute the comparison (or control) group. Quasi-experimental designs are those including a comparison group that has been chosen on the basis of matched characteristics but not random assignment.

An important bias of the literature is that mainly favorable outcomes are published, so it may not reflect a wider, possibly negative, body of evidence about the area of concern. However, there may also have been many programs that have contributed favorably to the health and well-being of children and families but were not reported in the literature. Many programs do not have an evaluation component, or many may have lost funding or faced other crises before their evaluations were completed. Finally, long-term follow-up evaluations necessitate a lapse of years between intervention and publication of results. In that time, the world may have changed enough to make it imprudent to uncritically apply the lessons learned to new interventions (Lazar and Darlington, 1982).

HISTORICAL REVIEW OF TARGETED EARLY INTERVENTION PROGRAMS

Many excellent and comprehensive reviews of the early intervention literature have been written since the 1960s, when early intervention programs began to proliferate (for recent reviews, see Meisels and Shonkoff, 1990; Seitz, 1990; Benasich, Brooks-Gunn, and Clewell, 1992; Olds and Kitzman, 1993; Barnett, 1995; Yoshikawa, 1995; Guralnick, 1997; Reynolds et al., 1997). These reviews can be differentiated based on the criteria the authors used for inclusion of studies in their analysis. Many reviews are oriented to a specific type of intervention or a specific age group or type of outcome. Other reviews use methodological criteria—including design, sample size, attrition, and length of follow-up period—to delineate the literature.

In the remainder of this chapter, we draw on the early intervention literature and previous reviews to highlight some of the most prominent targeted early intervention programs, with particular attention to studies potentially relevant to cost-savings analysis. In particular, we focus on ten programs:

- Early Training Project
- High/Scope Perry Preschool Project
- Project Head Start
- Chicago Child-Parent Center (CPC) and Expansion Program

- Houston Parent-Child Development Center (PCDC)

- Syracuse Family Development Research Program (FDRP)

- Carolina Abecedarian

- Project CARE (Carolina Approach to Responsive Education)

- Infant Health and Development Project (IHDP)

- Elmira Prenatal/Early Infancy Project (PEIP).

These programs share a common aim: to improve child health and development by providing socioeconomically disadvantaged children and their families with various services and social supports during part or all of the period of early childhood. Although most of these programs are considered "model programs," two have been implemented on a large scale—Project Head Start and the Chicago Child Parent Center and Expansion Program—and the Infant Health and Development Project was implemented at eight sites. The remaining programs were implemented at one site, although replications in other settings are under way for at least one program. Taken together, these ten programs have been some of the most influential in establishing an understanding of the effects of targeted early intervention programs.

We focus on these studies because they also meet several other criteria we believe are important for providing more-reliable estimates of both short-run and long-run program effects: experimental design, preferably with randomized assignment to treatment and control groups; a sample size of 50 children or more in treatment plus controls; a follow-up period, preferably past the period of program intervention; and less than 50 percent attrition at follow-up.[3] The ten programs that we review here do not exhaust those that would meet the criteria we list above.[4] Rather, our goal is to illustrate the range of

---

[3]Besides excluding studies with nonexperimental designs, small samples, no follow-up, or high attrition, we also do not focus on analyses of multiple studies. For example, the Consortium for Longitudinal Studies (Lazar and Darlington, 1982) conducted a collaborative follow-up for several early childhood programs, including the Early Training Project and the Perry Preschool program, which we review here.

[4]For example, Barnett (1995) reviews a longer list of programs using similar criteria, although his review does not include Project CARE, the Infant Health and Development Project, or the Prenatal/Early Infancy Project. By excluding other published

interventions that have been studied, highlighting the types of effects that have been measured for these representative programs. In the concluding section of this chapter, we take account of the broader literature and highlight any differences between the inferences we draw based on the ten studies featured here and those based on a more comprehensive review of the literature.

Table 2.1 provides information on the characteristics of the programs we review, including the place and time period of implementation, the characteristics of the intervention (i.e., target group; ages of participation; and the focus, mode, and nature of services provided), and the features of the evaluation (i.e., whether a randomized controlled experiment, initial and follow-up sample sizes, and the ages of the children at follow-up). The table and the discussion of the programs that follows highlight the diversity of these interventions. In part, the diversity arises from the differences in program objectives—program components are designed to mediate such different stressors in early childhood as low income, poor health, or lack of cognitive stimulation or emotional support. Design features that are affected by program objectives include how children are targeted for intervention, which members of the family receive program services or treatments, and the nature and mode of service delivery. As summarized in Tables 2.2 and 2.3, the variation in program objectives also leads to differences in the outcomes measured for children and their parents.

First, targeted early intervention programs may select participants using different criteria, with different definitions of which children and families are most in need—or most at risk of being exposed to stressors that might compromise development. Impediments to optimal child outcomes include impaired emotional relationships; insufficient cognitive stimulation; resource deficiencies associated with low income, poor nutrition, or inadequate access to health care; and, more controversially, linguistic and cultural factors. In the studies we review, the criteria for identifying children for treatment include being in a family with low socioeconomic status (SES), having a low IQ, or being born prematurely with a low birthweight.

---

studies from our review, we do not mean to imply that their results are necessarily biased.

Table 2.1

Features of Selected Targeted Early Intervention Programs

Program Years of Operation Site	Target	Intervention				Random Assignment	Evaluation Design		
		Ages of Participants	Focus	Mode	Content		Initial Sample Size	Sample Size at Final Follow-Up	Ages at Follow-Up
Early Training Project[a] 1962–1965 Murfreesboro TN	Low SES	Entry: 4 to 5 years Exit: 6 years	Child	Center/ home	Summer part-day preschool program. Home visits.	Yes	E=44 C=21	E=36 C=19	6, 7, 8, 10, 16–20
High/Scope Perry Preschool Project[b] 1962–1967 Ypsilanti, MI	Low SES and low IQ scores	Entry: 3 to 4 years Exit: 5 years	Child	Center/ home	School-year day preschool program. Home visits.	Yes	E=58 C=65	E=58 C=63	5–11, 14, 15, 19, 27
Project Head Start 1965–present multiple	Low SES	Entry: 3 years Exit: 4 years	Child	Center/ home	Preschool program. Home visits.	NA	NA	NA	NA
Chicago CPC[c] 1967–present Chicago, IL	Low SES	Entry: 3 to 4 years Exit: 6 to 9 years	Child/ parent	Center	Preschool: Half-day school-year program. School-age: Kindergarten and primary (to 3rd grade) programs.	No; statistical controls for nonrandom participation	E=1,150 C=389	E=878 C=286	9, 10, 11, 14
Houston PCDC[d] 1970–1980 Houston, TX	Low SES	Entry: 1 (HV); 2 (center) Exit: 3 years	Child/ parent	Home/ center	Home visits. Part-day child care. Center-based program for parents.	Yes	E=90 C=201	School data: E=50 C=87 Achievement tests: E=39 C=76	3, 4–7, 8–11

Table 2.1—continued

Program Years of Operation Site	Intervention					Random Assignment	Evaluation Design		
	Target	Ages of Participants	Focus	Mode	Content		Initial Sample Size	Sample Size at Final Follow-Up	Ages at Follow-Up
Syracuse FDRP[e] 1969–1975 Syracuse, NY	Low SES	Entry: last trimester (HV); 6 months (center) Exit: 5 years	Child/ parent	Home/ center	Home visits. Part-day (6–15 months) to full-day (15–60 months) year-round family-style day care.	No; matched comparison group selected at 36 months	E=108 C=108	E=65 C=54	5, 6, 15
Carolina Abecedarian[f] 1972–1985 one site in NC	High score on high-risk index	Entry: 6 weeks to 3 months Exit: 5 to 8 years	Child/ parent	Center	Preschool: full-day year-round center-based educational day care. School-age: parent program.	Yes	E=57 C=54	E=48 C=44	8, 12, 15
Project CARE[g] 1978–1984 one site in NC	High score on high-risk index	Entry: 4 weeks (HV); 6 weeks to 3 months (center) Exit: 5 years	Child/ parent	Home/ center	Home visits and full-day year-round center-based educational day care (E1). Home visits only (E2).	Yes	E1=17 E2=25 C=23	E1=14 E2=23 C=22	4-1/2
IHDP[h] 1985–1988 8 sites	Premature and low birthweight	Entry: birth (HV); 1 year (center) Exit: 36 months (adjusted for prematurity)	Child/ parent	Home/ center	Home visits. Full-day year-round center-based educational day care.	Yes	E=377 C=608	E=336 C=538	3, 5, 8

Table 2.1—continued

Program Years of Operation Site	Target	Ages of Participants	Focus	Mode	Content	Random Assignment	Initial Sample Size	Sample Size at Final Follow-Up	Ages at Follow-Up
Elmira PEIP[i] 1978–1982 Elmira, NY	First births to young, single or low-SES mothers	Entry: up to 30th week of gestation Exit: 2 years	Parent	Home	Home visits by trained nurses.	Yes	E=116 C=184	E=97 (mothers), 94 (children) C=148 (mothers), 144 (children)	3, 4, 15

NOTES: Age references are to the age of the focal child. E = experimental; C = control; HV = home visits; NA = not applicable.

[a]Gray and Klaus (1970); Gray and Ramsey (1982); Gray, Ramsey, and Klaus (1982); Lazar and Darlington (1982).

[b]Weikart, Bond, and McNeil (1978); Schweinhart and Weikart (1980); Berrueta-Clement et al. (1984); Schweinhart et al. (1993).

[c]Reynolds (1994, 1997); Reynolds and Temple (1995); Reynolds, Chang, and Temple (1997).

[d]Johnson et al. (1974); Andrews et al. (1982); Johnson and Breckenridge (1982); Johnson and Walker (1991).

[e]Honig and Lally (1982); Lally, Mangione, and Honig (1988).

[f]Ramey, Dorval, and Baker-Ward (1983); Ramey and Campbell (1984, 1991); Campbell and Ramey (1994, 1995).

[g]Ramey et al. (1985); Wasik et al. (1990).

[h]IHDP (1990); McCormick et al. (1991, 1993); Ramey et al. (1992); Brooks-Gunn et al. (1994a, b); McCarton et al. (1997).

[i]Olds et al. (1986a, 1986b, 1988, 1997); Olds, Henderson, and Kitzman (1994); Olds (1996).

A second feature of program design concerns which members of the family receive program services and during what period of child development. Among the programs summarized in Table 2.1, some concentrate resources on treating the parents—or more typically the mother—because changing the mother's behavior may improve the child's development (e.g., through improved emotional support, better cognitive stimulation, or an increase in economic self-sufficiency). Interventions that focus on the mother often begin during the prenatal period and continue through the early period of child development. Other programs focus on treating the child, often intervening during the period just before entering school—ages 3 and 4. As noted in Table 2.1, some programs combine these two approaches and treat both parents and children during different stages of early childhood.[5]

Third, the programs we review in Table 2.1 also vary in the location and nature of the services provided. Some programs offer services in the family's home, others provide services in a center setting—typically a child care center—and others may provide services in both. Guided by program objectives, the types of services often vary by whether they are provided to the mother or child, and whether they are provided in the home or a center setting. For instance, a program designed to improve child health might provide the mother training in parental skills in the home; for the child, there might be home-safety inspections and child-abuse recognition in the home and health screenings in a clinic. Another program that strives to promote school readiness might only provide services to the child in a center—such as social interaction and cognitive stimulation. Programs providing services for children in centers may also have the added objective of facilitating the mother's employment because they provide child care.

---

[5]Another model, called "two-generation" programs, adopts a three-pronged approach by providing adult-focused, parent-focused, and child-focused services. In these programs, family support and preschool education activities are combined with parent education and job training, the latter aimed at increasing economic self-sufficiency. Examples of large-scale programs include Even Start Family Literacy Program, New Chance, the Comprehensive Child Development Program, and the JOBS Child Outcomes Study. Smaller-scale examples include the Avance Family Support and Education Program. For recent reviews of these and other two-generation programs, see St. Pierre, Layzar, and Barnes (1995) and IRP (1997b).

Finally, as summarized in Tables 2.2 and 2.3, the benefits from targeted early intervention programs have been measured for children and their parents (largely for mothers) in four domains: emotional and cognitive development, education, economic well-being, and health.[6] As we highlight in the discussion that follows, gains in the child's cognitive or emotional development have been measured through improved behavior and higher IQ in the treatment versus the control group, although these gains typically erode soon after the intervention ends. Educational improvements have been observed for the child in several areas, including better achievement test scores, increased rates of school completion, faster promotion from grade to grade, and reduced participation in special education programs. Improvements in economic well-being have been measured for children, although these behavioral differences are not observed until later follow-ups when the child reaches adolescence or young adulthood. Finally, interventions have also produced health benefits for children, including reduced levels of child abuse and emergency room visits.

Our understanding of the effects of early intervention programs on a parent's behavior is more limited, since only a few of the studies we review include any assessment of parental outcome differences and then almost exclusively for the child's mother. Favorable benefits for mothers include more satisfactory parent-child relationships, improved educational attainment and labor force participation, reductions in welfare utilization and criminal behavior, and better health outcomes.

In the remainder of this chapter, we turn to a more detailed discussion of each of the ten programs summarized in Tables 2.1–2.3. Most of the programs we highlight were carried out in the 1960s and 1970s; a few began in the 1980s. Our discussion places these efforts in their

---

[6]As we discuss below, the numerous evaluations of Project Head Start are not readily summarized in the format used in Tables 2.2 and 2.3 (see Barnett, 1995, for a recent review of many of the Head Start evaluations). Thus, while we include Head Start in our review of historically important intervention programs, we have elected not to include Head Start in the tables that summarize program benefits. In addition, some of the studies we review collected information at follow-ups for other outcomes, including various attitudinal measures for children and parents. See, for example, those summarized for the Early Training Project (Gray, Ramsey, and Klaus, 1982) and the Perry Preschool Program (Berrueta-Clement et al., 1984; Schweinhart et al., 1993).

Table 2.2

Children's Measured Outcomes and Results for Selected Targeted Early Intervention Programs

Program	Cognitive and Emotional Development	Education	Economic Well-Being	Health
Early Training Project	IQ at age 6 (W): E>C E=95.0, C=82.8 IQ at age 7 (W): E=C E=97.7, C=91.3 IQ at age 17 (WR): E=C E=78.7, C=76.4	Achievement tests at age 7: E > C Achievement tests at age 10: E = C Achievement tests at age 17: E = C Special education by age 18: E<C E=3%, C=29% Grade retention by age 18: E=C E=58%, C=61% High school graduation rate by age 18: E=C E=68%, C=52% Complete high school after pregnancy by age 18: E > C E=88%, C=17%	NM	Teen pregnancy through age 18: E=C

Table 2.2—continued

Program	Cognitive and Emotional Development	Education	Economic Well-Being	Health
High/Scope Perry Preschool Project	IQ at age 5 (SB): E>C E=94.9, C=83.5 IQ at age 7 (SB): E>C E=91.7, C=87.1 IQ at age 8 (SB): E=C E=88.1, C=86.9 IQ at age 14 (W): E=C E=81.0, C=80.7	Achievement tests at age 9: E>C Achievement tests at age 14: E>C High school GPA at age 19: E > C Time in special education through age 19 (% of years): E<C E=16%, C=28% Years in educable mentally impaired programs through age 27: E=C E=1.1, C=2.8 Years retained in grade through age 27: E=C E=0.5, C=0.7 High school graduation rate by age 27: E > C E=65%, C=45% Postsecondary education credits by age 27: E=C E=33%, C=28%	Ever arrested by age 27: E<C E=57%, C=69% Lifetime arrests through age 27: E<C E=2.3, C=4.6 Employment rate at age 19: E>C E=50%, C=32% Employment rate at age 27: E=C E=71%, C=59% Monthly earnings at age 27 (1993 $): E>C E=$1219, C=$766 Received public assistance at age 27: E<C E=15%, C=32% Received public assistance in last 10 years at age 27: E<C E=59%, C=80%	Teen pregnancies per 100 females through age 19: E=C E=68 C=117
Chicago CPC	Teacher ratings of school adjustment at age 9: E=C	Achievement tests at age 9: E > C Achievement tests at age 14: E>C Special education by age 9: E=C E=8%, C=9% Special education (yrs) through age 14: E<C E=0 6, C=0.5 Grade retention by age 9: E<C E=19%, C=23% Grade retention by age 14: E<C E=25%, C=37%	Delinquency rate through ages 13–14: E<C Delinquency rate through ages 15–16: E=C	NM

Table 2.2—continued

Program	Cognitive and Emotional Development	Education	Economic Well-Being	Health
Houston PCDC	IQ (B) at age 2: E>C E=98.8, C=90.8 IQ (SB) at age 3: E=C E = 108.1, C=104.0 Behavior problems at ages 4–7: E<C	Achievement tests at ages 8–11: E>C Grades at ages 8–11: E=C Special education by ages 8–11: E=C E=14%, C=17% Grade retention by ages 8–11: E=C E=16%, C=23% Bilingual education by ages 8–11: E<C E=14%, C=36%	NM	NM
Syracuse FDRP	IQ (SB) at age 3: E>C E=110.3, C=90.6 IQ (SB) at age 6: E = C E=109.1, C=105.0 Socioemotional behavior at age 3: E>C Socioemotional behavior at age 6: E<C	Grades at age 15: E > C (girls only) Special education by age 15: E = C Grade retention by age 15: E = C Attendance at age 15: E > C (girls only) Teacher ratings at age 15: E > C (girls only)	Referred to probation by age 15: E<C E=6%, C=22%	NM
Carolina Abecedarian	IQ at age 5 (WP): E > C E=101.4, C=93.7 IQ at age 8 (WR): E > C EE+EC=97.8, CE+CC=93.3 IQ at age 12 (WR): E > C EE+EC=93.7, CE+CC=88.4 IQ at age 15 (WR): E = C EE+EC=95.0, CE+CC=90.3	Achievement tests at age 8: E > C Achievement tests at age 15: E > C Special education by age 15: E < C EE+EC=25%, CE+CC=48% Grade retention by age 15: E < C EE+EC=31%, CE+CC=55%	NM	NM

Table 2.2—continued

Program	Cognitive and Emotional Development	Education	Economic Well-Being	Health
Project CARE	IQ at age 1 (B): E1 > E2, C E1=119.3, E2=107.8 C=108.5 IQ at age 3 (SB): E1 > E2, C E1=104.5, E2=88.4, C=92.9 IQ at age 4.5 (M): E1 > E2, E1 = C E1=103.1, E2=89.9, C=96.0	NM	NM	NM
IHDP[a]	IQ at age 3 (SB): E > C E=93.6, C=84.2 IQ at age 5 (WP): E > C (HLBW only) E=95.4, C=91.7 IQ at age 8 (W3): E > C (HLBW only) E=96.5, C=92.1 Behavior problems at age 3: E<C Behavior problems at age 5: E<C (HLBW only) Behavior problems at age 8: E=C	Achievement tests at age 8 (math only): E=C (HLBW only) Grade repetition by age 8: E=C E=14%, C=15% Special education by age 8: E=C E=17%, C=20%	NM	General health at age 8: E=C

Table 2.2—continued

Program	Cognitive and Emotional Development	Education	Economic Well-Being	Health
Elmira PEIP[b]	IQ at age 3 (SB): E=C E=103.6, C=102.0 IQ at age 4 (SB): E=C E=111.5, C=108.9	NM	Arrests through age 15: E<C (HR only) E=0.24, C=0.53 Convictions through age 15: E=C E=0.13, C=0.18	ER visits, ages 25–50 months: E<C E=1.0, C=1.5 Hospital days, ages 25–50 months: E>C E=0.54, C=0.30

NOTES: Age references are to the age of the focal child. Results that are not statistically significant are designated by E = C; results that are significant at the 0.05 level or better are designated by E > C or E < C.

NM = not measured; E = experimental, C = control; for Carolina Abecedarian, the first letter indicates preschool treatment and the second school-age, e.g., EC = experimental during preschool, control at school age. For IQ tests: B = Bayley Mental Development Index; M = McCarthy Scales of Children's Abilities; SB = Stanford-Binet; W = Wechsler Intelligence Scale for Children; WP = Wechsler Preschool and Primary Scale of Intelligence; WR = Wechsler Intelligence Scale for Children–Revised; and W3 = Wechsler Intelligence Scale for Children–III.

[a]Results are for full sample unless otherwise indicated. Heavier low-birthweight (HLBW) infants are those born greater than 2,000 grams.

[b]Results are for full sample unless otherwise indicated. The higher-risk (HR) sample is defined as single mothers with low SES for child results through age 15.

Table 2.3

Parent's (Mother's) Measured Outcomes and Results for Selected Targeted Early Intervention Programs

Program	Emotional/Parenting Development	Education	Economic Well-Being	Health
Early Training Project	NM	NM	NM	NM
High/Scope Perry Preschool Project	NM	NM	NM	NM
Chicago CPC	Parental involvement in school at age 9: E > C	NM	NM	NM
Houston PCDC	Mother-child interactions at age 3: E>C HOME Inventory at age 3: E>C	NM	NM	NM
Syracuse FDRP	NM	Completed high school by age 5: E>C	NM	NM
Carolina Abecedarian	HOME Inventory at age 4-1/2: E=C	Years of education at age 4-1/2: E>C E=11.9, C=10.3	Employment/occupational status at age 4-1/2: E>C	NM
Project CARE	Childrearing attitudes at age 3: E1=E2=C HOME Inventory at age 4-1/2: E1=E2=C	NM	NM	NM
IHDP	Mother-child interactions at age 2-1/2: E>C HOME Inventory at age 3: E>C	Months in school through age 3: E = C E = 4.9. C=4.2	Months employed through age 3: E>C E=16.7, C=15.6 Months on public assistance through age 3: E = C E=14.4, C=12.6	Subsequent pregnancy through age 3: E=C

Table 2.3—continued

Program	Emotional/Parenting Development	Education	Economic Well-Being	Health
Elmira PEIP[a]	HOME Inventory at 46 months: E=C Reports of child abuse and neglect through age 15: E<C E=0.29, C=0.54	Years of education at age 4: E=C E=11.4, C=11.1	Months employed through age 15: E=C E=96.4, C=89.7 Months on AFDC through age 15: E<C (HR only) E=60.4, C=90.3 Months on Food Stamps through age 15: E<C (HR only) E=46.7, C=83.5 Months on Medicaid through age 15: E=C E=61.8, C=70.0 Arrests through age 15: E<C (HR only) E=0.18, C=0.58 Convictions through age 15: E<C (HR only) E=0.06, C=0.28 Jail days through age 15: E<C (HR only) E=0.04, C=1.11	Subsequent pregnancies through age 15: E < C (HR only) E=1.5, C=2.2 Subsequent births through age 15: E < C (HR only) E=1.1, C=1.6 Months between first and second birth through age 15: E > C (HR only) E=64.8, C=37.3 Substance use impairments through age 15: E<C (HR only) E=0.41, C=0.73

NOTES: Age references are to the age of the focal child. Results that are not statistically significant are designated by E = C; results that are significant at the 0.05 level or better are designed by E > C or E < C. NM = not measured; E = experimental; C = control. The HOME Inventory assesses aspects of parental care giving and characteristics of the physical home environment.

[a]Results are for full sample unless otherwise indicated. The higher-risk (HR) sample is defined as single mothers with low SES for mother results through the child's age 15.

historical context. This presentation of historically important interventions and their evaluations provides a basis for understanding the current policy debate regarding the future of investments in early childhood programs. Early intervention efforts today clearly echo the debates of prior eras. Reflection on the prejudices and limitations of earlier work may improve the outcomes of future efforts.

First Models for Targeted Early Intervention

Many historical accounts have been written about the early intervention programs that debuted in the 1960s (Zigler and Muenchow, 1992; Zigler and Styfco, 1993; Richmond and Ayoub, 1993). Here we discuss three of the most influential.

Early Training Project

Early intervention theory and practice today were shaped by the first efforts in the early 1960s at enhancing development in children with mental retardation thought to be caused by inadequate home environments. One of the initial large studies was the Early Training Project directed by Susan Gray in Murfreesboro, Tennessee (Gray and Klaus, 1970; Gray and Ramsey, 1982; Gray, Ramsey, and Klaus, 1982; Lazar and Darlington, 1982). The motivation for this program was concern over the progressive retardation of low-income children in school. The intervention was designed to improve academic performance through better cognitive performance and achievement orientation.

The Early Training Project enrolled 65 black children from the 1958 cohort selected from a low-SES sample based on parent occupation, education, and income, and on housing conditions. Participants were randomly assigned to the intervention (either a three-summer or two-summer program) or a control group. Between 1962 and 1965, those in the treatment group received weekly home visits during the school year and participated in a 10-week part-day preschool program during the summer. Children were assessed during the intervention period and in 1965, 1966, 1968, and 1975 at approximately ages 7, 8, 10, and 17, respectively. At the time of the final follow-up in 1978, most participants were 19 years old, with 80 percent of the original participants available for long-term outcome assessment.

Early results identified a significant difference between treatment and control groups in terms of IQ, but these effects disappeared within a few years.[7]   Differences in achievement tests were also significant in the first few years after the intervention: By the end of the first grade (in 1965), children receiving the intervention scored higher on three of four subtests of the Metropolitan Achievement Tests. However, by fourth grade (in 1968), the differences between the two groups of children, while in the expected direction, were no longer significant on this same test. In later follow-ups through the high school level, no significant differences were found between the experimental and control groups on a range of tests (including the WISC-R for intelligence and the Stanford TASK, a comprehensive achievement test).

Although the intervention did not produce lasting differences in IQ or achievement tests between treated and nontreated children, the evaluation did find that experimental children were less likely to ever be placed in a special education class (specifically, a class for the "educable mentally retarded"). Program participants were also less likely to be retained in grade or to have dropped out of high school, but the differences were not statistically significant. While treatment and control girls showed no significant difference in their rates of teen pregnancy, among the treatment group, those who bore children were significantly more likely to return to school and obtain their high school diploma.

High/Scope Perry Preschool Project

The High/Scope Perry Preschool Project in Ypsilanti, Michigan, provides one of the longest assessments of the effects of early childhood intervention for low-income children (Weikart, Bond, and McNeil, 1978; Schweinhart and Weikart, 1980; Berrueta-Clement et al., 1984; Schweinhart et al., 1993). Like the Early Training Project, the program was motivated by the poor school performance of economically disadvantaged children. By enrolling children in one or two

---

[7]Scores on the Wechsler Intelligence Scale for Children (WISC) were no longer significant at age 7 (Lazar and Darlington, 1982), while the Stanford-Binet scores remained significantly different until age 10 (Gray and Klaus, 1970).

years of preschool, the program aimed to improve cognitive and social outcomes in both the short and long run.

The initial preschool study consisted of 123 African American children and their parents who enrolled in the study over five waves
between 1962 and 1967.[8] The intervention group was gathered by
interviewing all families with 3-year-olds in Ypsilanti during each
project year. Families were rated on the basis of parent education,
occupation of head of household, and household density. For families who scored low on the rating of socioeconomic status, children
were administered an intelligence test. Each participant was assessed to have an IQ (Stanford-Binet) of less than 85 on entry into the
study.

Participants were randomly assigned to either the preschool program
or a control group. The only exceptions to random assignment were
younger siblings who were assigned to the same group as already
participating older siblings, and two children who were moved to the
control group because of parental conflicts with participation in the
preschool. The program participants were followed annually
through age 11, and again at ages 14, 15, 19, and 27, with data collected through interviews, school records, and public record reviews.
At the age 27 follow-up, 117 of the 121 living participants completed
interviews. Attrition of the study groups averaged about 9 percent
and was not significantly different between the treatment and control
groups, nor was attrition related to characteristics at program entry
(Barnett, 1993). The long follow-up for this study and the low rate of
attrition sets it apart from most others in the literature. The relatively
small sample sizes, however, are a drawback.

Over the course of the intervention, 45 children entered the Perry
Preschool at age 3 and attended for two years, while 13 entered at age
4 and attended one year before entering public kindergarten. The
study intervention consisted of daily 2-1/2 hour center-based classes
and weekly 90-minute teacher home visits, both delivered from October to May each year. The in-class teacher-student ratio was 1 to 6,
and all the teachers were certified public school teachers trained in
child development. The curriculum evolved over the five years of the

---

[8]Five children in the original sample of 128 children were lost because of migration or
death during the preschool treatment period.

study from a nursery school to a Piagetian-based early education approach (Barnett, 1993).

The study was well designed to provide information on a broad range of outcomes, including cognitive development, academic achievement, work activities, welfare participation, and criminal records (Schweinhart et al., 1993). Despite the small sample sizes, both short- and long-run assessments demonstrate favorable effects for children participating in the preschool program across a broad spectrum of outcomes (see Table 2.2).[9] As with other early intervention studies of the era, the first outcomes measured were changes in IQ. At the end of the program intervention, children in the preschool program had IQ scores that exceeded the control group by over 11 points. The favorable IQ effect for program participants began to decline after school entry, disappearing by second grade (age 8) (Schweinhart and Weikart, 1980).

These early favorable IQ effects were followed by improved academic achievement even after differences in IQ between the groups ceased to be statistically significant. For instance, achievement test scores for program participants remained significantly higher than those for the control group through age 14. Preschool participants had better grades and were more likely to have graduated from high school; at age 28, however, there were no differences in postsecondary education participation (Schweinhart et al., 1993). Time in special education was significantly lower for program children at ages 19 and 27. The difference in grade retention, while in the expected direction, was not significant at age 27.

At the last follow-up, other lasting differences were evident as well in employment, welfare, and crime outcomes (Schweinhart et al., 1993; Barnett, 1993). For instance, by age 27, program participants had significantly lower rates of current and past welfare utilization (i.e., AFDC—Aid to Families with Dependent Children, Food Stamps, general assistance, and so on). Lifetime criminal activity—both incidence and severity—was also significantly lower. Employment rates and earnings for program participants were correspondingly higher,

---

[9]Results have been reported for other measures in addition to those summarized in Table 2.2, including other economic and social behaviors and attitudes (see, e.g., Berrueta-Clement et al., 1984; Schweinhart et al., 1993).

although the employment rate difference was statistically significant at age 19 but not at age 27.   Health effects, in contrast, were not as strong. The difference in the teen pregnancy rate by age 19 was large (64 per 100 females versus 117) but only marginally significant (p = .08).[10]   Other life course behaviors include a statistically significant higher rate of marriage by age 27 among women participants in the preschool program (Schweinhart et al., 1993).

The Perry Preschool program, because of its design, is often closely associated with the Head Start program, an intervention model we turn to next.   However, it is important to keep in mind that Perry differed in many respects from the average Head Start program as implemented today.   For instance, staff ratios were lower and instructors more highly qualified and trained. At the same time, the Perry Preschool program experienced some of the same problems evident with Head Start programs. For instance, average attendance was 69 percent in the first year and home visit appointments were also missed (Barnett, 1993).   Nevertheless, the study of long-term outcomes in Perry Preschool has been closely aligned with Head Start in an attempt to promote the benefits of early intervention and to draw attention to the effects of investments in program quality (Zigler and Muenchow, 1992).

Project Head Start

The most well-known of all early intervention programs, and certainly one of the largest, is Head Start. Initially designed and implemented as Project Head Start in 1965, its chief architects included child development experts Julius Richmond and Edward Zigler. The project was the result of a combination of factors, including public and policymakers' concern about the growing number of children living in poverty in the United States (Zigler and Muenchow, 1992; Richmond and Ayoub, 1993). The development of new theories of child development and the existence of a federal budget surplus also coincided with the program's initiation. Despite the limited experi-

---

[10]The birth rates are calculated based on the total number of pregnancies and live births per woman in treatment and control groups by age 19. The 24 women in the control group had a total of 28 births in contrast to 17 births for the 25 women in the treatment group.

ence with early intervention for socioeconomically disadvantaged children without disabilities, this large-scale program was launched.

At the time of Head Start's creation, the influence of Bloom and Hunt's theories regarding early developmental vulnerability and opportunity from environmental inputs coincided with political forces targeting government resources for altering the course of multigenerational poverty. The "cultural deficit" model of early intervention was predominant among policymakers and many social activists. It equated economic disadvantage with failure to provide the proper middle-class child-rearing experiences necessary for advancement in society (Swadener and Lubeck, 1995). Early intervention was seen as an inoculation against exposure to the detrimental influences of poverty, and it was believed to improve intelligence and lead to academic success (Lazar and Darlington, 1982; Ramey, Dorval and Baker-Ward, 1983).

Political circumstances had led to a budget surplus under the Economic Opportunity Act of 1964. Sargent Shriver, director of the Office of Economic Opportunity, was anxious to use the surplus funds for a program targeted at children (Cravens, 1993). The Kennedy family's experience with mental retardation had led them to create a foundation for research on mental retardation that included support of early education programs for economically disadvantaged children with retarded development. Shriver had been greatly impressed by a visit with his wife, Eunice Kennedy Shriver, to the Early Training Project, which the Kennedy Foundation had sponsored (Zigler and Muenchow, 1992). Shriver hoped to create a national program that would achieve the same improvements in IQ as shown by the children served by the Early Training Project.

Shriver assembled a committee of child development experts to make recommendations for a model program for low-income children. These experts included the psychologist Urie Bronfenbrenner, who had just begun to elaborate his ecological theory of child development (Richmond and Ayoub, 1993). The ecological perspective examines how a child's interactions with environment and society affect developmental outcomes. This was one of the first theories to model early childhood development not as a linear, cause-and-effect process, but rather as the confluence of many different layers of environmental factors (Meisels and Shonkoff, 1990). Bronfenbrenner's theories were influential in the design of Head Start and subsequent early childhood interventions.

Program Implementation. As originally conceived, Project Head Start was an experimental eight-week pilot project implemented in 1965 in nearly 2,500 communities across the country, with the goal of improving the social competence of economically disadvantaged preschool children. The first trial served 500,000 4- and 5-year-old children and their families and was launched within 12 weeks of the announcement of the experimental initiative (Zigler and Muenchow, 1992). The intervention was designed to be comprehensive, with a home-visit as well as a center-based component. It provided social, health, and education services in addition to early education opportunities. Parental participation was integral to the program.

The popular and political appeal of Project Head Start, however, was based on public attention to the possibility of raising IQ scores in children rather than on its broader goals (Zigler and Muenchow, 1992). It was thought that early intervention would raise intelligence and lead to improved life outcomes for poor children (Ramey, Dorval, and Baker-Ward, 1983). The comprehensive nature of the intervention was likewise underemphasized in policy arenas at the time of its implementation and during evaluations years later.

As Zigler and Muenchow point out in their account of Head Start's implementation, there were few paradigms for early childhood programs in the United States in 1965 (Zigler and Muenchow, 1992). Only 18 states had public kindergarten programs, and there was almost no experience with preschool education. The planning document for the project had few guidelines about educational activities and requirements for training preschool staff. Head Start has been handicapped by and criticized for this lack of attention to quality of services, curriculum, and staffing; and reforms of Head Start in the 1970s began to address such quality issues.

The Head Start program has changed considerably since 1965. In its second year of funding, many programs expanded to a nine-month, half-day service, and by the early 1970s most programs were designed as school-year programs (Zigler and Muenchow, 1992). There continued to be an emphasis on local parent and community involvement in addition to national program standards. This resulted in considerable program variation across localities (Zigler and Styfco, 1993).[11]

Many other child and family support programs were developed as a result or extension of the Head Start experience. Parent and child centers (PCCs) were launched by the Head Start Bureau in 1967 in 33 communities across the country. They were created to address the concerns that Head Start began too late in development to be effective. The PCCs were designed to serve low-income families with children up to 3 years of age through the provision of comprehensive health, social, and educational services. Project Follow Through was designed to provide continued intervention into middle childhood and addressed concerns at the other end of Project Head Start's time spectrum—when vulnerable children enter the public school system without continued support. It was thought that continued intervention in elementary school would provide long-lasting IQ effects (Zigler and Muenchow, 1992).

Other Head Start programs include Education for Parenthood, which provides parenting education for adolescents; Parent and Child Development Centers, designed to study infant development and parenting; and Child and Family Resource Programs, a service center for families with children to age 8. More recent programs include the Head Start Migrant programs, Comprehensive Child Development Centers, and Early Head Start. The latter two programs are models of comprehensive family support programs for low-income families with children under 5 years of age.[12]

Program Evaluation. The Head Start program has served over 15 million children at a cost of $31 billion since 1965 (GAO, 1997). There is a huge volume of literature that reflects the continued interest in the design and outcomes of investments in this program. An evaluation of Head Start research literature released this year by the General Accounting Office found nearly 600 citations and documents on

---

[11]Head Start providers are public and private agencies that apply for grants from the Department of Health and Human Services to cover 80 percent of program costs, with the remaining 20 percent obtained from nonfederal sources (GAO, 1997).

[12]For a recent review of these and related programs, see St. Pierre, Layzar, and Barnes (1995).

Head Start (GAO, 1997).[13] In the discussion that follows, we first focus on evaluations of Project Head Start. Because the program has been the subject of numerous other evaluations since that time, we provide a brief review of those assessments as well.

Measuring the success of Head Start is complicated by several factors. First, there has been no national randomized control trial conducted for purposes of evaluating the program as originally designed.[14] Thus, researchers have had to overcome the lack of an experimental design, which continually raises concerns over possible biases due to analytic methods. Second, the widespread implementation of the program and changes in design and program regulation over the years means that there is no single program to evaluate. Program services have varied from place to place and in response to the changing profile of the low-income children and families served.

Finally, the earliest assessments were constrained by both popular and academic attention to cognitive achievement despite the wider goals of the Head Start program. Researchers were handicapped, in part, by limited experience in the early 1960s in evaluating early childhood interventions. While methodology for studying cognitive outcomes was well developed, early evaluators had little experience or literature to guide them in the measurement of less tangible changes in child and family behaviors. This bias toward examining primarily cognitive effects continued with later assessment, as well (Currie and Thomas, 1995).

The earliest evaluations of Project Head Start, based on the program first implemented in 1965, showed some promising results, including changes in IQ as large as 10 points for the first summer program participants (Deutsch, 1967; Zigler and Muenchow, 1992). A study of a group of New York children in this first summer program assessed school readiness and found that Head Start participants were initially

---

[13]As we noted earlier, the many studies evaluating Head Start are not easily summarized in the same format as the other programs reviewed in Tables 2.2 and 2.3. Consequently, Head Start is not included among the programs summarized in those tables.

[14]Some experimental studies with randomized treatment and control groups have been conducted. However, their small samples, nonrepresentative study populations, and possible nonrandom attrition may have produced biased estimates of the effects of the overall program (Barnett, 1992, 1995).

better prepared for school, but that these effects faded within a few months (Wolff and Stein, 1966). These assessments were hampered, however, by the lack of experimental design and limited resources to measure outcomes other than IQ.

To improve upon these early assessments, a national evaluation of Head Start's first three years was commissioned by the Johnson administration. The Westinghouse Report (Cicirelli, 1969) was intended to provide—in the shortest amount of time possible (little more than a year)—a national assessment of the first three years of the Head Start effort. It used a national sample of children, with 70 percent drawn from the first summer Project Head Start participants and 30 percent from the subsequent full-year program participants. These children were matched retrospectively with a control group, and cognitive effects using standardized measures were assessed. There was also an unsuccessful attempt to assess child attitudes in school using unvalidated measures.

The Westinghouse analysis did not find any favorable cognitive effects from participation in the summer program (Cicirelli, 1969). It did find that in first and second grade, full-year participants performed better on a school readiness test, but the researchers were unable to draw conclusions about third grade performance because of the small sample size. There were also geographic and ethnic subgroup variations in performance. Based on these results, the study concluded that Head Start was not beneficial. However, the study's design, with its retrospective control group, raised serious concerns regarding the legitimacy of its conclusions. Though this design flaw could not be overcome through analytic methods, later reanalyses of this study with improved statistical modeling of the participants and control groups did find small favorable effects from the summer program, although researchers continue to debate the size of the effect (Barnow and Cain, 1977; Bentler and Woodward, 1978; Magidson and Soerbom, 1982).

The Westinghouse report coincided with a reversal in the political and societal climate of the early 1960s, which led to a shift of government priorities away from social service programs (Honig and Lally, 1982; Zigler and Muenchow, 1992). Many longitudinal early intervention studies and services such as Head Start and Project Follow

Through experienced draconian budget cuts or ceased to exist during this period (Reynolds, 1994; Honig and Lally, 1982).

At about the same time, Arthur Jensen published his monograph on genetic influences on IQ scores, emphasizing the dominance of nature over environmental influences on intelligence. He predicted that early intervention could not be successful because it is targeted at children whose potential is limited by genetics (Jensen, 1969). While his premises were controversial, the monograph served to reinforce a stigma on Head Start's first efforts at early intervention for economically disadvantaged children. Disenchantment with Head Start was also fostered by the Coleman Report, which concluded that schools were unable to overcome the socioeconomic circumstances of children participating in compensatory education programs and that the quality of early education experience had little effect on school outcomes (Coleman et al., 1966).

In 1971, Bronfenbrenner was commissioned by the Office of Child Development to review the early intervention literature to date. He also concluded that short-term benefits of program participation fade in elementary school within two to three years (Brontenbrenner, 1974). In his report, he reemphasized the importance of family in fostering and sustaining development, and pointed to family-focused interventions as the remedy for academic "fade-out." The broader implications of his conclusions were not emphasized as much as his evaluation of the long-term effects of early intervention.

A decade later, in 1981, the Administration for Children, Youth and Families funded an in-depth review of the Head Start literature and findings called the "Head Start Evaluation, Synthesis and Utilization Project" (McKey et al., 1985). This meta-analysis reviewed over 210 reports on Head Start and 1,600 other related documents to produce a synthesis of outcomes of the first 20 years of Head Start. The final analysis was based on 76 studies that met eight broad selection criteria (McKey et al., 1985). These criteria did not include sample size, attrition, or random assignment design, and the meta-analysis is unable to account for possible intrinsic biases in the results of the original studies that are due to these factors. These limitations must be kept in mind when considering the findings of the study.

The meta-analysis, like many studies that preceded it, concluded that there were immediate cognitive benefits of participation in Head Start but that these benefits did not persist over the long term. However, based on a limited number of studies, Head Start participants were found to have better school success in terms of grade retention and special education use. Socioemotional gains were also found to be favorable but possibly transitory as well. There were definite, favorable physical health effects found.

More recent analyses have measured the effects of Head Start participation using alternative statistical methods and a broader array of outcome measures. For example, Currie and Thomas (1995) use data on children from the National Longitudinal Survey of Youth (NLSY), a nationally representative sample, to estimate the effect of Head Start on school performance, cognitive attainment, access to preventive medical care, and health and nutritional status. They find, for white children, that Head Start has significantly favorable and lasting effects on test scores and school attainment relative to participating in other preschool programs or no preschool program. Significant favorable increases in test scores for black children are also measured at young ages, but these gains eventually disappear. For both white and black children, Head Start is associated with higher immunization rates but no differences in long-run nutritional status as measured by child height-for-age.

The Next Generation of Targeted Early Intervention Programs

Early intervention models in the 1970s evolved as researchers and service providers became more cognizant of the role of family, culture, and society in child outcomes. The conclusions of the first Head Start studies that emphasized the overwhelming effect of the parents and home on an intervention's effectiveness helped shape the family intervention models that followed in the 1970s. Bronfenbrenner's ecological model of development was well known, and there was a better understanding of the interaction of the child with family and environment. Consequently, many of the model programs in this period were designed to intervene even earlier in childhood, with parents as a focal point as well as the child. Interventions and their evaluations were designed with an eye to disproving

Jensen's theory and the negative conclusions of the Westinghouse study (Honig and Lally, 1982). Below we discuss five of the most prominent early intervention programs initiated during the 1970s.

Chicago Child-Parent Center and Expansion Program

The Chicago Child-Parent Center (CPC) was started in 1967 in 11 Chicago public schools to serve economically disadvantaged children age 3 to 5 years (Reynolds, 1994, 1997; Reynolds and Temple, 1995; Reynolds, Chang, and Temple, 1997). With federal funds (through Title I, now Chapter I), the preschool program initially provided a structured half-day program during the nine-month school year for 3- to 4-year-olds, and was designed as an early education program to prepare children for school through promotion of reading and language skills. The program provided comprehensive services including health and social services and parent involvement. In 1978, with additional state funding, the program was expanded to continue services for children through third grade, including a full-day kindergarten component. Today, 24 centers provide preschool and postschool components, through grades 1, 2, or 3.

Outcomes for one recent cohort of CPC children have been followed in the Longitudinal Study of Children at Risk (LSCR), a prospective study of the adjustment to school of 1,539 low-income minority children (95 percent black, 5 percent Hispanic) in 26 Chicago-area kindergarten programs.[15] The LSCR provides an opportunity to evaluate the CPC program using a quasi-experimental design, comparing outcomes for the 1,150 participants in 20 CPCs having both preschool and after-school components with those from a control group of 389 nonparticipants in six randomly selected schools having a locally funded, full-day kindergarten program for low-income children. Children in the control group did not have access to a CPC in their neighborhood. Children in the LSCR form a single age cohort, entering the program at age 3 or 4 (1983–1985) or kindergarten (1985–1986), graduating from kindergarten in the spring of 1986. Some children continued to participate in the CPC through age 9 (1989) for a total of up to six years in the intervention. At the time of

---

[15]This study is also sometimes called the Chicago Longitudinal Study (Reynolds, 1997).

the latest follow-up at age 14, about 75 percent of both the treatment and the follow-up groups are available for study. Data on the children's outcomes include achievement tests from school records, and interviews with teachers, parents, and children to assess scholastic, social, and psychological development.

Unlike Head Start, the CPCs are integrated with the primary schools: The preschool and kindergarten programs meet in buildings of their affiliated elementary schools. While the curriculum is not uniform across centers, they all aim to provide comprehensive health, social, academic, and school support services to promote school readiness, with a special emphasis on reading and language skills and parental involvement. During the preschool years, children attend a structured half-day program during the nine-month school year; the kindergarten consists of a full-day (six hour) school-year program. The primary grades program provides reduced class sizes, parental involvement activities, and instructional coordination. Other comprehensive services at each age include free breakfasts and lunches, and health screenings. Adult-to-child ratios average 1 to 8 and 1 to 12 for the preschool and kindergarten components, with class sizes of 17 and 25, respectively. Average class sizes for the control children in kindergarten and primary grades was 30.

Examining data covering the preschool, kindergarten, and primary grades, researchers have used psychometric and econometric techniques designed to account for the nonrandom participation of children in the CPC—through controls for relevant background variables and explicit modeling of the selection mechanism (Reynolds, 1994, 1997; Reynolds and Temple, 1995). Because children entered the program at different ages and participated for varying lengths of time in both preschool and postschool intervention, it is possible to examine the effects of the timing (i.e., entry point) and duration of treatment on outcomes, albeit without the advantage of a randomized control design.

At the end of the intervention at age 9, those who participated in the CPC had significantly higher reading and math achievement scores, lower rates of grade retention and higher ratings of parental involvement. There were no significant differences found, on average between participants and nonparticipants, in special education placement and teachers ratings of school adjustment at age 9, although years of special education were significantly lower for treatment children by age 14 (Reynolds, 1994, 1997). The differences in achievement scores between groups tended to become smaller over time although they remained significant through age 14 for math scores. The findings for regression-controlled mean differences are generally similar to those based on models that explicitly consider selective program participation (Reynolds and Temple, 1995).

A comparison, based on time in the intervention, across children showed strong duration effects: At age 14, six-year program participants had the largest gains compared with nonparticipants in terms of reading and math scores, grade retention, and years of special education (Reynolds, 1997). For most of the outcomes studied through age 9, the association between time in the program and program benefits, rather than being linear, exhibited a threshold effect: Those who participated four years or more had the greatest benefits (Reynolds, 1994). Moreover, the results indicate that participation in both preschool and primary grade components confers the greatest benefits. Results based on data through age 14 suggest that, controlling for duration in the program, there were no significant differences between those who began with the preschool versus the kindergarten component.

Finally, researchers have recently examined measures of problem, illicit, or illegal behavior in grades 7 to 10 (Reynolds, Chang, and Temple, 1997). While differences in delinquency rates between treatment and control groups based on time in the program were significant at ages 13 to 14, these differences were no longer evident at ages 15 to 16.

Houston Parent-Child Development Center

The Parent-Child Development Centers (PCDCs) were an outgrowth of the CPCs. The PCDCs were among the first attempts by the Office of Economic Opportunity (OEO) to evaluate models of improving child outcomes through family intervention customized to individually assessed needs. The Houston PCDC was one of OEO's model research and demonstration projects designed to promote parental change by educating a sample of low-income Mexican-American mothers as well as their children (Johnson et al., 1974; Andrews et al., 1982; Johnson and Breckenridge, 1982; Johnson and Walker, 1991).[16] To address the concern that Head Start services started too late, the Houston PCDC provided services beginning when children were 1 year old.

Program participants were recruited from Houston neighborhoods with the lowest levels of family income and adult education, and high concentrations of Mexican Americans. Mexican American families with a child age 1 year old were randomly assigned to treatment or control groups. Families were recruited across eight cohorts to participate in the program between 1970 and 1980. To date, results are available for the first five cohorts through a follow-up when the children were between the ages of 8 and 11 (Johnson and Walker, 1991). Attrition rates have been very high, with only about 50 percent of the original sample available for follow-up. A comparison of sample characteristics at the latest follow-up shows no evidence of bias due to selective dropout or follow-up attrition, but the high attrition rate is problematic nonetheless. Preliminary results are available for a more recent follow-up, when the oldest children were age 16 (Institute for Research on Poverty, 1997a).

In the first year of the program, a paraprofessional educator made an average of 25 home visits designed to provide the mother with improved skills in teaching her infant, especially in the area of language development. In the second year, mothers and children were treated in a center setting for up to four half-day sessions per week. At the center, mothers participated in a curriculum that emphasized child cognitive and language development and other aspects of child rearing, health, and safety. Children were in a Piagetian-based nursery school while their mothers attended these classes. English language classes were also available to mothers on a voluntary basis. Fathers were encouraged to participate as well through weekend sessions during the first and second years.

---

[16]In the initial phase, from 1970 to 1975, the PCDC program was also implemented in Birmingham, Alabama, and New Orleans, Louisiana. For initial results of these programs, which differed to some extent from the Houston model, see Andrews et al. (1982).

At the earliest follow-up, children in the program (first two cohorts) were found to have higher IQ scores. But the difference, which was significant at age 2, was only marginally significant (p < .10) by age 3 (Andrews et al., 1982). Mother-child interactions and the home environment, predictors of later behavior problems, were better in the treatment group at age 3. Behavior problems, which were measured at ages 4–7 (first four cohorts), were also significantly better for the treatment group (Johnson and Breckenridge, 1982). By the time the children were ages 8 to 11, those who participated in the intervention had a decreased need for bilingual education services, with 14 percent of experimental children versus 36 percent of control children enrolled in bilingual education at the time of the follow-up survey (Johnson and Walker, 1991). Although achievement test scores were significantly higher for the treatment group at the same age, there were no significant differences in grade retention, special education referral, or school grades. Preliminary results at ages 9–16 show no differences in delinquency rates for program participants versus controls (IRP, 1997a).

Syracuse Family Development Research Program

The Family Development Research Program (FDRP) was implemented from 1969 to 1975 in Syracuse, New York. It consisted of adding intensive, comprehensive family services, including home visits by paraprofessionals starting prenatally, to the already established early education and child care program at Syracuse University (Honig and Lally, 1982; Lally, Mangione, and Honig, 1988). The intention of the intervention was to improve the quality of life for the children and their mothers. It was hoped that these adjunctive services would give rise to better parenting and home environment—and improved parental autonomy and self-sufficiency—and would lead to improved outcomes for the participating children.

At the outset of the FDRP, 108 families, mostly African American, were enrolled. These families had low income (less than $5,000 a year in 1970 dollars), and the family head had less than a high school education and only semi-skilled employment experience, if any. Eighty-five percent of mothers were single parents, and the mean age was 18 years. The design of the study was not randomized. A control group matched for age and sex with the FDRP children was recruited three years into the intervention.

Evaluation of the intervention was limited by loss of funding for long-term follow-up after the children completed second grade. Funding was eventually obtained for a follow-up that focused on collecting information for the treatment and control groups through interviews with the child, parents, and teachers, and through records from schools and various components of the criminal justice system. Of the original 108 families in the intervention, 82 completed the full program, and 65 (60 percent of the original enrolled sample) consented to follow-up at 14 years. Of the control group, 74 completed the study and 54 (50 percent of the original control group) provided consent for the 14-year follow-up. Interviews with parents and children were actually completed for a smaller sample in each group (51 and 42 parents and 49 and 39 children in treatment and controls, respectively). Although the attrition rates are high, the follow-up treatment and control samples did not differ significantly on a series of observed indicators from the group that completed the program. Nevertheless, sources of potential bias include nonrandom attrition associated with unobserved factors and the delayed matched-control design.

Families participating in the intervention received information about child nutrition, health and safety, and social services, starting in the third trimester of pregnancy and continuing until the intervention children reached 5 years of age and entered school. Weekly home visits provided an ongoing assessment of service needs and referrals in the community as well as parenting and child development education. Parents in the intervention participated in the program design and delivery through a formal parent organization similar to that of the Head Start model. The intervention was run in conjunction with the Syracuse University Children's Center preschool program that offered year-round, quality day care; the center provided a specialized curriculum of early education for the infants and children enrolled in the intervention. From 6 to 15 months, infants were cared for in a half-day day-care setting, with a ratio of four infants to one caregiver. Preschoolers from 15 to 60 months attended a full-day, family-style day-care program that emphasized development of social as well as cognitive skills through an unstructured learning environment.

In the short term, the study found differences in IQ and language skills between the groups, with an IQ advantage at age 3 nearly equal to 20 points. While the treatment group still maintained a significant IQ advantage at age 4, by age 6 the difference was small and no longer significant (Honig and Lally, 1982). Socioemotional behavior in the intervention group was observed to be superior at 5 years of age but was actually inferior during first grade. It was postulated that the public school experience produced this effect because of its contrast with the quality preschool educational experience (Lally, Mangione, and Honig, 1988). Positive effects for mothers were also reported, with more intervention mothers than control mothers completing high school during their five-year participation (Honig and Lally, 1982).

In the age-15 follow-up, the study found that there was a statistically significant advantage in school attendance and grades among girls who completed the program, relative to those in the control group. Boys in the intervention did not score higher on these measures than those in the control group, and there were no differences in other educational measures between intervention and control groups for either gender. Rates and severity of juvenile delinquency, as measured by Probation Department records, were significantly lower for the treatment group compared with controls (Lally, Mangione, and Honig, 1988).

Carolina Abecedarian

The Carolina Abecedarian project was started in 1972 at the Frank Porter Graham Child Development Center of the University of North Carolina (Ramey, Dorval, and Baker-Ward, 1983; Ramey and Campbell, 1984, 1991; Campbell and Ramey, 1994, 1995). The goal of the intervention was to prevent mild mental retardation and improve academic and social competence at school entry for economically disadvantaged children. Specifically, the study was designed to examine the relative effects of day-care early education and other methods of early intervention on intellectual functioning and early academic achievement among the most disadvantaged families. In contrast to the other studies we have reviewed thus far, the Abecedarian program began just weeks after the child's birth, with a high-quality educational day-care program.

Families were recruited between 1972 and 1977 from prenatal clinics and social service agencies for participation on the basis of their scores on a "High-Risk Index" that examined demographic and psychosocial factors thought to contribute to school failure. Other criteria in the index included level of parental education, income, intelligence, and antisocial and maladaptive behaviors in the family. While 122 families identified met the criteria, the final sample consisted of 109 families (because of refusals and the exclusion of several children for mental retardation and nonrandom reassignment to one of the treatment groups); 111 children from those families were enrolled in the study. The resulting sample was 98 percent African American, with mothers who were age 20 on average, and mostly single, with a first-born child. The children were randomly assigned by 6 weeks of age to either the preschool intervention or a control group. At age 5, at the time of kindergarten entry, all the children were reassigned to either school-age intervention through age 8 or a control group. Of the original 111 children, 92 were followed until age 15.

The day-care/preschool educational program was a full-day, year-round, center-based intervention with an infant/toddler-to-teacher ratio of 3 to 1, and a child-to-teacher ratio of 6 to 1. Special curricula were developed for each age group, including a transitional program for the children entering the kindergarten intervention group. Children also received medical services at the center. The intervention program during the primary grades consisted of providing the children with extra exposure to academic concepts by having their parents engage in specific supplemental educational activities at home. A home/school resource teacher (HST) provided parents with curriculum material and other support about every two weeks (13 to 15 times a year on average), in addition to other parental support and advocacy with school staff. On alternating weeks (14 to 18 times a year on average), the HST visited the child's classroom so that materials could be customized based on the school curriculum and the child's progress.

At the end of the preschool intervention, the treatment group significantly outperformed the controls in terms of IQ, with a 7 point difference in the Wechsler Preschool and Primary Scale of Intelligence (Ramey and Campbell, 1991). IQ scores at 8 years of age continued to be significantly higher for the preschool participants than for the other children (Ramey and Campbell, 1991). Most notable, four years after the intervention at age 12, this favorable and significant difference was also found; but the difference, while favorable, was no longer significant by age 15 (Campbell and Ramey, 1994, 1995). The study design, with treatment groups that experienced only the preschool intervention, only the postschool intervention or both, demonstrated that the strong and longer-lasting IQ effects derived from the preschool component of the intervention; in other words, the postschool intervention had little effect on the IQ differences observed between treatment and control samples.

Although the IQ effects diminished with time, at age 15, children who had participated in the preschool program still had significantly higher scores on tests of reading and mathematics, effects that had also been observed at ages 8 and 12 (Campbell and Ramey, 1995). They also had less grade retention (significantly different at ages 8, 12, and 15) and less special education placement (significantly different at age 15 only). The persistent achievement test and education outcome results, in contrast to IQ, were attributable in part to the intervention that continued after primary school entry. These results are suggestive of a role for high-quality, educational, center-based care in promoting early cognitive development, combined with subsequent school-age intervention to boost academic performance.

Finally, maternal interviews when the child was 54 months old showed that treatment mothers had significantly more years of education (after having had no difference at the start of the intervention) (Ramey, Dorval, and Baker-Ward, 1983). In addition, mothers in the program were also less likely to be unemployed and more likely to have a skilled or semi-skilled job.

Project CARE

Project CARE (Carolina Approach to Responsive Education), also at the University of North Carolina, was designed as a follow-up study to the Abecedarian Project (Ramey et al., 1985; Wasik et al., 1990). This time, home-based early intervention was tested in addition to the center-based, educational, day-care program examined in the original study. The experimental design was structured to allow comparisons between more and less intensive early educational treatment programs.

Starting in 1978, 65 families participated in the study and were randomly assigned to intervention services that lasted five years. Families were recruited from local hospital records of births over an 18-month period and screened using the High-Risk Index. Over 90 percent of the sample children were black, and about three out of four were from single-parent households. Mothers on average were age 22, and 60 percent were first-time mothers. All but one of the families agreed to participate in random assignment to (1) home visiting, (2) center-based intervention and home visiting, or (3) the control group. Families in the intervention groups began receiving home visits one month after the child's birth, and the center-based intervention began between 6 weeks and 3 months of age. One death and the relocation of four families reduced the sample size to 59 families by the end of the study, when the children were age 54 months, an average attrition rate of just under 10 percent.

Like the Abecedarian program, the center-based program consisted of full-day, year-round, educational day care, with low staff-to-child ratios and a well-structured curriculum. The family education component involved home visits by a trained family educator (usually the day-care teacher for children in the center-based program) about two and one-half times per month for the first three years and less frequently in years four and five (slightly more than one visit per month on average). Most visits (over 90 percent) were with the mother and lasted about an hour. Through child learning activities, the educators focused on child development, as well as on training in family problem-solving and parental skills. Parents in both intervention groups received additional child-rearing support and information about community resources through monthly workshops. All treatment and control children benefited from free iron-fortified formula through 15 months of age, as well as access to free medical care and other social services in the Chapel Hill area.

Children were assessed at 6- to 12-month intervals for five years using standardized tests of development, intelligence, and home environment and parenting. The strongest cognitive outcomes were found in the children who received the center-based services as well as home visiting. While the three groups showed no difference in cognitive tests at 6 months, by 1 year the children who received both day care and home visits had significantly higher scores than either the other treatment group (home visits only) or the controls (Ramey et al., 1985). The advantage of this group over the other two grew smaller as the children approached 5 years of age, and it is theorized that this was a benefit of the participation of the home-visit only and control groups in community day care (Wasik et al., 1990). The group receiving family education alone never showed significant differences in cognitive outcomes compared with the control group. The three groups did not differ over the course of the study in the degree to which the home environment was judged conducive to development or in terms of child-rearing attitudes (Wasik et al., 1990).

More Recent Models of Targeted Early Intervention

Guided by the results of the model programs developed in the 1970s, and the ongoing evaluations of even earlier interventions, researchers have continued to design and evaluate alternative targeted intervention programs. More recent efforts have used alternative criteria to identify families and children at risk. However, the focus on intervention at the earliest ages continued, with programs that started with the birth of the child, if not earlier. Evaluations were more carefully designed to incorporate larger samples in both experimental and control groups (which permits stratifying results by factors thought to be associated with risk), and long-term follow-up. In addition, more recent studies examine an expanded range of outcomes for both participating children and their families. Two of the better-designed recent interventions are discussed here.

Infant Health and Development Project

The Infant Health and Development Project (IHDP) built upon the work of the Abecedarian and Project CARE studies but targeted infants who were born prematurely (less than 37 weeks gestation) and with low birthweight (less than 2,500 grams) (IHDP, 1990; McCormick et al., 1991, 1993; Ramey et al., 1992; Brooks-Gunn et al., 1994a, 1994b; McCarton et al., 1997). Such children are considered at risk for long-term intellectual difficulties and delayed development. The focus on biological risk, which may be strongly associated with socioeconomic risk, sets this program apart from the others we have discussed.

The study was a multisite randomized clinical trial designed to assess the efficacy of educational and family support services in preventing cognitive deficits in this population. Infants were enrolled in the study during a nine-month period in 1985 and were selected from infants born at eight participating medical institutions. Among the 4,551 infants identified as eligible based on birthweight and gestation, 3,249 were excluded for the following reasons: home too great a distance from the intervention site, physical exam consistent with greater than 37 weeks of gestation, or discharge before or after the designated recruitment period. Of the remaining group, 274 parents refused to participate, and 43 withdrew after randomization. The final sample size was 985 infants in the treatment and control groups with a sample that was about 50 percent black and 10 percent Hispanic. At the time of the last follow-up at age 8, 874 children were available for follow-up, about 90 percent in each of the groups.

The intervention began after discharge from the hospital and continued until the infant reached 36 months (corrected for prematurity). All children in both the intervention and control groups received medical, developmental, and social assessments, with referral for further care as indicated. The intervention participants also received (1) home visits weekly for the first year and then biweekly for an average of 67 visits over three years; (2) a full-day, year-round, center-based, educational day-care program starting at 12 months of age with average attendance of 267 days per year over both years; and (3) a series of parent group meetings every other month in years two and three. The primary outcome measures were cognitive development, behavioral competence ranked by the mothers, and health status. Long-term outcome measures at 8 years of age also included a standardized measure of academic achievement and parental report of school performance.

The outcomes of the IHDP are reported in aggregate and separately for the heavier birthweight infants (those greater than 2,000 grams) and the lighter birthweight infants (those less than 2,000 grams). (Tables 2.2 and 2.3 report results for the full sample, noting when results hold for only the heavier low birthweight infants.) At the end of the intervention at (adjusted) age 36 months, the participants had significantly higher IQ scores than the controls—by nearly 10 points—with the greatest difference in the heavier birthweight children. The intervention group also had higher receptive vocabulary test scores on the developmental measure, and lower scores on maternal reports of behavior problems (Ramey et al., 1992). At 5 and 8 years of age, the significant differences in IQ were no longer apparent for the combined treatment group, although the heavier birthweight infants still had significantly better IQ scores than their matched controls (Brooks-Gunn et al., 1994a; McCarton et al., 1997). At age 8, no differences were found in rates of grade repetition or special education, or in terms of behavior problems or child health status. Math achievement scores were significantly different for the heavier birthweight group only.

Studies of the effects of the intervention on maternal outcomes have also been reported. Intervention group mother-child interactions at 30 months of infant age were judged significantly better (by a small margin) than those in the control group (Spiker, Ferguson, and Brooks-Gunn, 1993). Mothers in the intervention group were employed more months during the three years of the intervention and returned to work earlier than the control group mothers (Brooks-Gunn et al., 1994b). At the same time, there were no significant differences in welfare utilization or months in schooling over the three years, or in the rates of subsequent pregnancy.

Other analyses examined outcome differences based on participation rates and various risk factors. At 2 and 3 years of age, children in those families with the best participation in intervention services had better scores on the cognitive and development measures than those whose participation levels were lower (Blair, Ramey, and Hardin, 1995). Among poor families, the size of the effects of the program varied with the number of risk factors: larger effects for those with none to four risk factors, but no effects for those with six or more risk factors (Liaw and Brooks-Gunn, 1994). In addition to poverty, the risk factors examined included biological indicators (low birthweight, neonatal health), socioeconomic factors (race/ethnicity, parental unemployment, and mother's characteristics such as education, verbal ability, and mental health) and family structure (teenage mother, single parent).

Prenatal/Early Infancy Project

The Prenatal/Early Infancy Project (PEIP) conducted by researchers at the University of Rochester was a study of the effects of home visiting on economically disadvantaged first-time mothers and their children. The study was conducted from 1978 to 1982 in Elmira, New York, and long-term follow-up on the children and their mothers is available for children at age 15 (Olds et al., 1986a, 1986b, 1988, 1997; Olds, Henderson, and Kitzman, 1994; Olds, 1996).

Five hundred first-time mothers were recruited between 1978 and 1980 from prenatal clinics and social service agencies, and 400 were enrolled in this study before their 30th week of pregnancy.[17] Women recruited for this study were those who were thought to be at high risk for poor child and family outcomes, although to avoid stigmatization, any first-time mother who asked to participate was accepted. Among the 400 participants, 85 percent had at least one of the following sociodemographic risk factors: less than age 19 at registration (48 percent), unmarried (62 percent), or low socioeconomic status (SES) (59 percent). Nearly one in four participants had all three risk factors.[18]

Participants were stratified by marital status, race, and geographic area, and were randomly assigned to one of the two intervention or two control groups. One intervention group received home visiting only during pregnancy, and the other received home visits until the children were two years old. Both intervention groups and one of the control groups received free transportation to prenatal and well-child visits. The only service that the other control group received was health and developmental screening at 1 and 2 years of age, with appropriate follow-up referrals. Differences between treatment and control group outcomes focus on the treatment group that received both prenatal and early infancy home visits (N = 116) versus the two control groups combined (N = 184).

The intervention groups were visited by registered nurses trained in parent education, methods of involving family and friends in assisting and supporting the mother, and linkage of the family with other health and human services. These services were provided to pro-

---

[17]There were no differences in age, marital status, or education between the study participants and the 100 women invited to participate but who were not enrolled.

[18]Because of the low number of minority women in this population and study (N = 46), minority participants were excluded from some analyses of maternal and child effects through age 4 of the children.

mote maternal functioning with respect to health-related behaviors during pregnancy and infancy, parental caregiving, and maternal life-course development (e.g., family planning, education, and employment). The targeted developmental processes were based on an ecological/systems model focusing on parental behaviors and social environment as important influences on pregnancy and child health outcomes. On average, nurses completed 9 visits during pregnancy (about 1 hour and 15 minutes every two weeks) and 23 visits from the child's birth to age 2.[19]

Data were collected at registration, at 32 weeks gestation, and then every four to six months for four years, with a final follow-up when the child was 15 years old. At that time, both mother and child were interviewed, and attempts were made to review state criminal and social service records for data on the mother. Reports of child abuse and neglect were also abstracted from archived state records. Of the original 300 women in the control and treatment groups described above, 245 mothers and 238 children completed assessments when the child was 15. At the final follow-up, results were reported for the full treatment plus control sample, as well as for a subsample of unmarried, low-SES mothers (samples sizes for treatment and control groups of 38 and 62, respectively).[20]

The study found significant short- and long-term advantages for both the mothers and children in the intervention group. In the short term, pregnancy behaviors were better for mothers in the intervention group, with less cigarette use, better nutrition, improved childbirth class attendance, and more social supports reported (Olds et al., 1986a). Mothers who smoked bore 75 percent fewer preterm infants than control mothers who smoked; overall, intervention group teenager mothers bore heavier infants than the control group teenagers did.

---

[19]Following birth, nurses initially visited approximately weekly up to 6 weeks of age, then every two weeks from 6 weeks to 4 months, every three weeks from 4 to 14 months, every four weeks from 14 to 20 months, and every six weeks from 20 to 24 months. The postnatal visits lasted a similar length of time (Olds et al., 1993).

[20]We note in Tables 2.2 and 2.3 when the results for the Elmira PEIP hold only for the higher-risk sample in the treatment and control groups. This occurs for child arrests and several of the mother outcomes when the child was 15, where the higher-risk sample is defined as unmarried low-SES mothers (Olds et al., 1997).

The program assessment through when the child was age 4 showed parental caregiving was also affected by participation in the intervention. There were decreased reports of child abuse and neglect during the first 2 years of life among the higher-risk families in the intervention group (Olds et al., 1986b). Fewer safety hazards and more development-promoting materials were found in the homes of the intervention group, and through age 4, these children were seen less frequently in the hospital emergency department (Olds et al., 1986b; Olds, Henderson, and Kitzman, 1994). Hospital days were significantly higher for the children through age 4 in the intervention group, although this results from one outlier in the sample that appears unrelated to the program (Olds, Henderson, and Kitzman, 1994). Through age 4 for the children in the treatment and control groups, no significant differences in IQ, completed years of education for the mother, or home environment were found (Olds et al., 1986a; Olds, Henderson, and Kitzman, 1994).[21]

The 15-year follow-up study found fewer reported acts of child abuse and neglect among the nurse-visited mothers for the full sample and the higher-risk sample (Olds et al., 1997). The other significant findings were restricted to the higher-risk sample (i.e., unmarried and low-SES mothers). For this group, months spent receiving AFDC and Food Stamps were significantly lower. The most at-risk mothers also had lower levels of criminal activity (measured by both self and state-documented data on arrests, convictions, and jail days) and reported fewer behavioral impairments due to alcohol and drugs. Although the full treatment group also spent fewer months receiving Medicaid and more months employed, the differences were not statistically significant. The beneficial effects of the program in terms of subsequent fertility continued through the 15-year follow-up, with higher-risk treatment mothers reporting fewer subsequent pregnancies and births, and a longer birth interval between the first and second child. Finally, children in the intervention group reported fewer arrests compared with those in the control group (Olds, 1996).

---

[21]For the subsample of poor, unmarried teens, the children in the treatment group, at ages 1 and 2, had IQ scores that exceeded those of the control group by about 10 points, although the difference was only marginally significant ($p < .10$) (Olds et al., 1986b).

The Elmira PEIP has been replicated for first-time mothers in a number of other communities for more diverse at-risk populations, specifically urban and minority samples. Randomized control trials began in 1990 for a sample of 1,139 low-income, unmarried, primarily African American women in Memphis, Tennessee, and in 1994 for a racially and ethnically mixed sample of 735 low-income, mostly unmarried women in Denver, Colorado. In early results for the Memphis trial, program participants demonstrated significantly lower levels of pregnancy-induced hypertension and reduced rates of subsequent pregnancies and injuries to their children through the age of 2 (Kitzman et al., 1997). Welfare utilization was also lower among program participants after two years, although the difference was only marginally significant (p < 0.10). There were no significant differences in children's mental development or behavioral problems, or in the mothers' education and employment. These findings track those exhibited for the Elmira sample after the first few years of the program (Olds et al., 1986a, 1986b). These samples are expected to be followed in the future so that researchers can continue to measure differences as the children mature.

SUMMARY OF FINDINGS

Given the shortcomings and limitations in the design of many early intervention evaluations and the measures omitted from them, what we don't know about the effects of early childhood intervention may exceed what we know (for more on this, see Chapter Four). Nonetheless, our review supports the proposition that, in some situations, carefully targeted early childhood interventions *can* yield measurable benefits in the short run and that some benefits persist long after the program has ended.

Moreover, as seen in Tables 2.2 and 2.3, many of the effects measured in the studies we review are sizable. For example, the Early Training Project, Perry Preschool, and IHDP found IQ differences between treatment and control groups at the end of program implementation that approached or exceeded 10 points, a large effect by most standards. The difference in rates of special education and grade retention for children at age 15 in the Abecedarian project exceeded 20 percentage points. In the Perry Preschool program, participating children had earnings that were 60 percent higher than those of the control group when they reached age 27. There was a 33 percent difference between participating and nonparticipating mothers in the Elmira PEIP in months spent on welfare during a 15-year period. The reduction in children's crime, measured in terms of probation cases by the Syracuse FDRP, was about 70 percent. While these findings are compelling, not all of the effects measured in the studies we reviewed here or reported elsewhere in the literature are as large, and there are many statistically insignificant results (as well as a few significant results that do not conform to expectations).

Figures 2.1 and 2.2 provide one way to further summarize what we have learned from the preceding review of selected early intervention programs. For each of the studies covered in Tables 2.2 and 2.3, we note whether the evaluation measured an outcome in that domain, and if so, whether the program led to favorable and statistically significant results, to no statistically significant results, or to mixed results.[22] In particular, the white squares indicate cases in which a study did not measure the outcome designated in that column. Dark gray indicates that the outcome was measured and was favorable and significant. Black shows that an outcome was measured but that the program had no effect (or, rarely, had a significant unfavorable effect). Light gray shading denotes those cases where results are mixed. This arises when favorable effects are found at one time but not at another (as in several studies for three of the four domains for children) and when multiple measures of crime or welfare utilization at a point in time show mixed results (as in several cases for children and mothers). Given that the ages at follow-up vary across studies and for particular measures, we also record in the dark gray and black squares the oldest age at which the measure is taken (which, for dark gray squares, also denotes the latest age at which a significant difference has been found). In the gray squares, we record only the oldest age at which a significant difference was found (there may have been subsequent measures yielding nonsignificant differences).

Given the interest in cognitive benefits from early intervention, we separately record whether a program produced IQ benefits in the

---

[22]Some outcomes reported in Tables 2.2 and 2.3 but that are measured in only one study are not shown in Figures 2.1 and 2.2.

short run (assessed at the end of the program intervention), and the results for longer-term IQ assessment. The long-run IQ result is sometimes mixed, with initial favorable benefits after program implementation eventually fading. This is illustrated by a gray box (where the age shown is the latest with a significant effect). Likewise, we show achievement test scores separately for short- and long-run measures.[23] Finally, the two figures show two sets of results for the IHDP (Figure 2.1 only) and the Elmira PEIP, first for the full study sample, and second for the subsample with stronger results. In the case of the IHDP, this is the heavier low-birthweight infants, a group that showed longer-lasting IQ and achievement test results. In the Elmira PEIP, the results for economic and health outcomes of mothers and crime outcomes for children are stronger for single mothers with low SES.

We now turn to a discussion of the general patterns that emerge from these figures, first for children and then for mothers. We link these conclusions to the larger literature on early childhood intervention.

Outcomes for Children

Most of the studies we reviewed measured effects for children, in some cases exclusively. In Figure 2.1, we first note that every study produced at least one significant benefit for the intervention children, whether in the short or long run, and most programs produced benefits in more than one domain. While we cannot attach weights to the areas that are dark gray or light gray versus black, a simple count reveals that there is more dark gray and light gray than there is black. Most measured effects are thus favorable.

Second, the dark gray areas are not limited to the first few columns. Early intervention programs affect more than just cognitive development, even when that is the main motivation behind an intervention's design. For example, there are often strong and lasting effects in terms of educational outcomes, with differences that

---

[23]For those programs that ended prior to age 5, we record achievement scores only as a long-run effect since they are typically first measured five or more years after the intervention has ended.

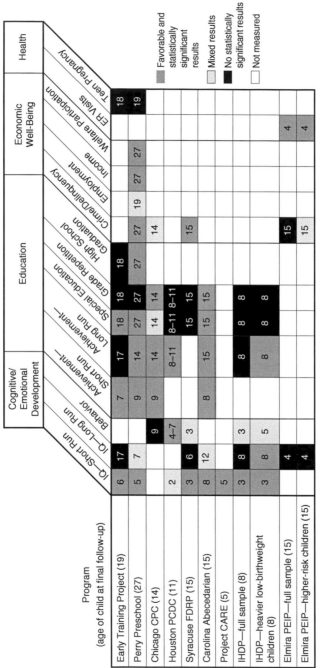

Figure 2.1—Effects of Selected Early Intervention Programs on Participating Children

SOURCE: See Table 2.2.

NOTE: Number in box refers to age of child when measure was last taken. When results were mixed (light gray squares), the age refers to the last age when the effect was significant. See text note for full program names.

continue throughout the school years. This finding is replicated in a number of other smaller-scale studies, as well as in pooled analyses of experimental programs (see Lazar and Darlington, 1982).

Third, there are even more white squares than filled squares. This means that most studies did not attempt to measure most of the outcomes, or that the follow-up has not been long enough to observe outcomes in many domains. As we will see later, this has implications for the cost-savings analysis: Savings for most programs will be understated because many potential benefits—especially those that can be readily monetized—were not, or have yet to be, measured.

Fourth, the benefits from early intervention programs have been measured for a diverse array of programs. Benefits are found for model programs as well as for interventions implemented on a larger scale. Significant findings are associated with programs that provide only home visits in the first few years of life, with those that offer only preschool programs for one or two years before school entry, as well as with all of the hybrid programs in between. When drawing conclusions about program benefits, it is important to keep in mind the considerable variation in the nature of the programs summarized in Figure 2.1. The programs differ from each other in such salient features as the age at program entry, duration of the intervention, the nature and quality of the services provided, and the mechanism for targeting at-risk children. With a few exceptions, it is not possible to sort out the contribution of any one of these particular design features to the strength or weakness of a particular study's findings.

These four observations, however, do not consider the variation across the domains featured in the tables. We conclude by highlighting those differences.

Cognitive and emotional development. As our review of these nine studies has demonstrated, the favorable effects in the IQ category must be interpreted with caution. Despite the recent attention on the critical period of brain development during the early years, early intervention programs—even those that provide services in the first few years of life—have been limited in their ability to demonstrate persistent cognitive effects, and the same is true for the measures of child behavior. While all of the studies in Figure 2.1 that measured IQ found significant differences during the intervention period or at the end of the treatment, these gains disappear within a few years after the end of the program services. This conclusion is consistent with the results from other programs that we have not focused on here.[24] One of the few exceptions, the Abecedarian program—which showed significant IQ effects for children measured at age 12, four years after the end of the intervention—offers some promise that very-high-quality center-based care in the early years can produce longer-lasting cognitive benefits.

Educational outcomes. Although the IQ effects produced by early intervention programs may be short lived, there appear to be strong and longer-lasting benefits in terms of educational outcomes, such as academic achievement and other aspects of school performance. While some early intervention models, such as the IHDP and Early Training Project, found achievement effects that disappeared by the time the children reached ages 8 and 10, other programs, such as the Perry Preschool, the Chicago CPC, and the Carolina Abecedarian programs, show gains at least through age 14 or 15 (although the gap in achievement scores also tends to narrow with time).[25] When rates of special education and grade repetition or retention are reported, outcomes are always better for the treatment group, although the gap is not always statistically significant. High school graduation rates are also higher for program participants, but children have been followed long enough to observe school completion in only two cases.[26] The results from the Chicago CPC and Abecedarian eval-

---

[24]See for example, the results from the Consortium for Longitudinal Studies (Lazar and Darlington, 1982) and the other model programs and large-scale interventions reviewed by Barnett (1995) and Reynolds et al. (1997). The Milwaukee Project, which provided high-quality, full-day educational child care through age 5, is one of the only other model programs to show longer-lasting IQ effects (through age 14). It was excluded from our review because of small sample sizes (N = 20 in treatment and control groups).

[25]Of the eleven model programs with achievement data reviewed by Barnett (1995), five measured achievement test gains beyond the third grade. Two of the five programs are the Abecedarian and Perry Preschool programs reviewed here. The other three programs are the Florida Education Project, the Harlem Training Project, and the Verbal Interaction Project.

[26]Again, these conclusions are similar to those reached by Barnett (1995) based on a review of 15 model early intervention programs and 21 large-scale public early intervention programs. In a "review of reviews," Reynolds et al. (1997) also conclude that "there is substantial support for longer-term effects on children's development,

uations suggest that the gains in academic success measures may be stronger the longer the duration of the intervention program and when preschool and postschool intervention components are combined.

Criminal activity. Only four of the nine programs summarized in Figure 2.1 attempted to measure crime and delinquency behavior among youth when they were followed at older ages. In the four cases where assessments have been made, the results are generally favorable, with lower incidence and seriousness associated with juvenile offenses of those in treatment versus control groups.[27] These four programs vary in the mode, nature, and timing of service delivery, although the stronger results appear to be associated with programs that provide both high-quality day-care or preschool programs and family support services (Yoshikawa, 1995).

Employment, income, and welfare participation. Follow-up for most study participants has not been long enough to observe key economic benefits in terms of labor force activity and reliance on the social safety net as adults. The Perry Preschool program is the one exception among the studies we list in Figure 2.1, and the results are very promising. Nevertheless, until other studies are able to follow treatment and control children into young adulthood, we must attach considerable uncertainty to the ability of early intervention programs to produce differences in economic outcomes at older ages.

Health outcomes. Given the explicit focus in many programs on providing health-related services to children, it is surprising that so few programs seek to measure health benefits for children in either the short or long run.[28] The lack of long-term follow-up also pre-

---

especially for school competence (e.g., children are less likely to be retained in grade and placed in special education)" (p. 7).

[27]A recent review by Yoshikawa (1995) of over 40 early intervention programs found only 4 that explicitly measure juvenile delinquency outcomes. At the time of his review, results for the age-15 follow-up were not yet available from the Elmira PEIP. In addition to the three others we list in Figure 2.1, the fourth program identified with positive benefits in this domain was the Yale Child Welfare Project, an intervention excluded from our review because of its small sample size (N = 18 in treatment and control groups).

[28]The IHDP assessed general health status, an outcome that is not specifically classified in Figure 2.1.

cludes examining other life-course health outcomes, such as child-bearing, an effect that is measured but not significant in either the Early Training Project or Perry Preschool program.

In sum, the effects of early intervention programs on children's outcomes appear to be strong in the domains of cognitive development and educational outcomes. While cognitive gains are substantial during or at the end of the intervention, they are often short-lived. However, even though IQ effects fade, other academic milestones show a greater tendency for sustained benefits. The focus on cognitive and academic measures is consistent with the motivation and design of the programs we reviewed. Other outcomes, such as economic well-being and child health, have not been assessed to the same extent—either because the follow-up period has been too short or because other factors, such as design considerations and resource constraints, led to a concentration on other outcomes.

Outcomes for Mothers

Figure 2.2 summarizes program effects on mothers. Here, in contrast to the results for children, significant favorable effects are balanced by those that are insignificant or mixed. But unmeasured outcomes dominate this figure even more than they did in Figure 2.1. While seven of the nine studies measure parental outcome in the domains covered by Figure 2.2, only four of the nine studies measure outcomes beyond parenting behavior.

Parenting. Comparisons across studies in this domain are difficult, given different measures for assessing the nature and quality of parenting. Among the studies reported in Figure 2.2, the results are mixed regarding the extent to which parenting is improved as measured by the quality of the home environment. Only one study each found benefits measured by parent-child interactions, parental involvement in schooling, or reports of child abuse and neglect. Other studies show similar results.[29] In many cases, regardless of the suc-

---

[29]Benasich, Brooks-Gunn, and Clewell (1982) found that 5 studies of the 27 they reviewed measured the quality of the home environment; only 2 studies found significant effects (the Houston PCDC and one other). Results for mother-child interactions were more favorable, with 10 of 11 programs that measured this outcome finding beneficial effects in program participants' favor.

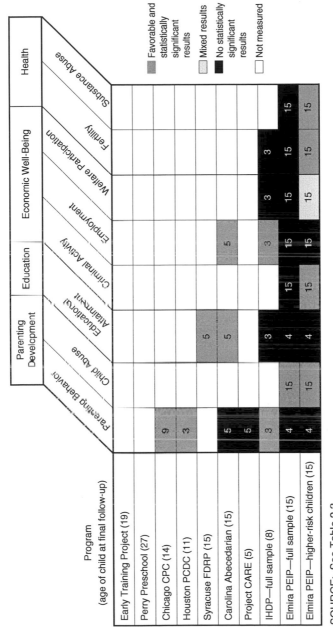

RAND*MR898-2.2*

SOURCE: See Table 2.3.

NOTE: Number in box refers to age of child when measure was last taken. When results were mixed (light gray squares), the age refers to the last age when the effect was significant. See text for full program names.

Figure 2.2—Effects of Selected Early Intervention Programs on Participating Mothers

cess of the intervention, the home environment and quality of parenting will exert a critical influence on children's outcomes. In the Carolina Abecedarian program, for example, there was little reason to expect that the quality of the home environment for learning would be different among treatment and controls (and indeed it was not as of age 5). Nevertheless, the home environment predicted cognitive test scores for both treatment and control groups (Martin, Ramey, and Ramey, 1990). Thus, for the Abecedarian sample, the home environment remained an important influence on children's cognitive outcomes in addition to the role of the day-care intervention.

Education and economic well-being. Even fewer studies focused on maternal education and economic outcomes. Among the four programs that measure the mother's educational achievement, two find a favorable effect when the child was 5: the Syracuse home visits and day-care program and the Abecedarian day-care program. The results for employment and welfare utilization are also mixed. Mothers in the IHDP had a significantly higher level of employment (one month on average) during the three years of the intervention, while mothers in the Abecedarian program had better employment outcomes (i.e., occupational status) when the child was almost age 5. The Elmira PEIP mothers also had more months of employment over 15 years (about 7 months for the full sample and 16 months for the higher-risk sample) but the differences were not statistically significant. While the IHDP mothers showed no differences in months on public assistance during three years, mothers in the Elmira PEIP had significantly lower levels of utilization for AFDC and Food Stamps but not Medicaid. To a large extent, these results mirror those in the early intervention literature, as well as in the job training literature.[30] While evaluations have found that job training programs are largely ineffective for other segments of the population, they indicate that disadvantaged adult women benefit in terms of higher annual earnings and lower welfare participation (U.S. Department of Labor,

---

[30]A recent review of 27 home- and center-based programs providing early intervention services during the first 3 years of life found favorable effects on maternal employment in 10 of the 11 studies that measured the outcome, although the magnitude of the effects were modest (Benasich, Brooks-Gunn, and Clewell, 1992). Fewer studies examined public assistance utilization.

1995); for some programs, the reduction in welfare payments out-weighs the cost of the training programs (Gueron, Pauly, and Lougy, 1991).[31]

Health. Among the studies summarized in Figure 2.2, the favorable health findings for mothers are limited to the Elmira PEIP, and there the benefits accrue only to higher-risk mothers. Most notable are the lower pregnancy and birth rates 15 years after the birth of their first child and the longer birth spacing between pregnancies. Given the explicit focus of the nurse home visits on maternal prenatal health behavior and postnatal life-course decisionmaking, these findings may not be replicated in other interventions that emphasize other services or alternative modes of service delivery.[32]

Given these findings, it is unfortunate that our understanding of the effects of early intervention programs on parental outcomes is so limited. Even when the child's parents are not the focus of the inter-vention, there may still be spillover benefits in terms of the parents' behavior. For example, programs that provide high-quality child care may increase the workforce participation of the mothers com-pared with mothers whose children do not participate in the pro-gram. As we will see in the next chapter, these improvements in par-ents' outcomes, while important in their own right, may also be important for establishing whether programs generate savings that exceed their costs.

---

[31]For reviews of the job training literature, see Reville and Klerman (1996); U.S. Department of Labor (1995), LaLonde (1995), and Grubb (1995).

[32]Benasich, Brooks-Gunn, and Clewell (1992) cite four programs in addition to the Elmira PEIP (two center-based programs and two home-based programs) that produced beneficial effects in terms of lower birth rates for participating mothers. They also find four out of a total of five programs produced beneficial effects for participants on measures of maternal mental health and self-esteem. The review of home-visiting programs by Olds and Kitzman (1993) suggests that effects on maternal life course and other maternal and child outcomes are likely to be stronger for home-visit programs that provide more comprehensive services by well-trained nurses or other professionals.

Chapter Three

COMPARING COSTS, SAVINGS, AND BENEFITS

Up to this point, we have examined the effects of early childhood intervention programs in terms of the benefits produced for children and their families. Some people may think that those benefits are enough to justify public expenditures on such programs. Others may appreciate the benefits to disadvantaged children but may be reluctant to raise their tax burden to accomplish such goals or may wish, at least, for broader favorable ramifications from an investment of public funds. In this chapter, we discuss some of these broader ramifications and show how some publicly funded early interventions may yield monetary returns in excess of their costs.[1]

To begin, consider some of the benefits of early intervention programs to individuals other than the child and his or her immediate family. For example, a program that reduces the amount of crime committed by a treated child also lessens the victimization experienced by other people. These other people enjoy abated loss from crime, primarily in the form of decreased property losses and less pain and suffering. If a program reduces the incidence of unhealthy behaviors in later life, such as drinking in conjunction with driving, everyone's insurance premiums—in this case, for automobile and possibly health insurance—could go down. Benefits also accrue more subtly. For example, an entire classroom of schoolchildren is better off if those class members who are less cognitively able are

---

[1]The cost-savings analysis reported in this chapter draws on previous assessments for both the Perry Preschool program (Barnett, 1993) and the Elmira PEIP (Olds et al., 1993). Our contribution beyond these earlier analyses are highlighted in the discussion that follows.

brought up to the level of the others. These indirect benefits that accrue to other individuals must be included when one considers the total value of such programs.

Benefits can also accrue to society at large. A principal recipient of such benefits is the government.[2] If a program results in higher earnings for a program participant, the government collects greater tax revenue. If a program participant is less likely to use welfare, the government's welfare outlays are reduced. Both ways, taxpayers are better off, either by receiving a larger collective benefit per dollar paid or, potentially, by receiving the same benefit from a reduced tax burden.

If it were possible to include and monetize *all* the benefits of a program, one could generate a complete cost-benefit ratio. However, monetizing many of the benefits of early childhood intervention is difficult or impossible. It is difficult, for example, to monetize the benefits of improved behavior or IQ, either for the child or for other members of the child's family or classroom. We cannot attach a monetary value to a mother's greater satisfaction with her relationship with her child. Neither can we determine at this time the monetary value to society of greater academic achievement on the part of children participating in early interventions. The same goes for many of the health benefits realized. Furthermore, benefits that can be monetized may result in future benefits that cannot. For example, if early intervention means that a child will be more economically successful as an adult (a monetizable benefit), that adult's children may not be exposed to the same stressors he or she was (a benefit that is difficult to monetize).[3] In this chapter, we restrict ourselves to benefits that can be easily monetized.

Since the government is likely to be the funder for large-scale early childhood programs, it is interesting to ask whether public expenditures for such programs could be justified, at least in part, by the sav-

---

[2]"The government" is sometimes used as a term separate from, even set in opposition to, "the people." We do not intend that here. Throughout this chapter, "the government" should be understood as the agent spending the taxpayers' money on their behalf, or simply as the public accounts of the people.

[3]In some cases, benefits that cannot be easily monetized themselves (e.g., IQ gains) may be linked to other benefits that, when measured, can be monetized (e.g., higher earnings in adulthood).

ings to government they generate. If the savings generated by such programs are greater than their costs, government fiscal support for such programs may be considered a worthwhile investment of public funds. Thus, we devote most of our attention to costs and savings to the government, since we can more comprehensively account for those than we can for the costs and benefits to society at large. In the discussion that follows, we refer to this analysis as *cost-savings analysis*, to differentiate it from more traditional *cost-benefit analysis*. (The latter takes into account the benefits that accrue to other members of society, both program participants and nonparticipants.)

This is not to say that programs for which the measured costs are greater than the measured savings should not be funded by the government. Early childhood intervention programs might be deemed worthy even if their costs exceed their savings to government, because not all of their benefits can be monetized. For this reason, measured net savings to the government should not be the sole basis for deciding whether to fund a program or which of a set of competing programs to fund. However, positive net savings should help allay the concerns of those troubled by the potential budgetary burden of government-funded early intervention.

Our principal objective, then, is to determine if early childhood intervention programs have the potential to save more money than they cost. We do this by analyzing two programs documented in the literature that are amenable to such a cost-savings analysis. Those two programs are the Elmira Prenatal/Early Infancy Project (PEIP) and the Perry Preschool.[4] That we judge only two program evaluations amenable to cost-savings analysis is worth some emphasis. It reflects the paucity of measured outcomes, the attrition problems, and other problems discussed in the review of the literature in Chapter Two.[5] It also suggests the need for more comprehensively

---

[4]In the Perry Preschool case, our analysis is limited to adaptation of Barnett's previous cost-savings analysis (Barnett, 1993) for comparability with our Elmira PEIP estimates.

[5]This observation and similar assertions in this chapter and elsewhere in this report should not be taken as criticisms of those designing and carrying out programs we judged not amenable to cost-savings analysis. Designers and implementers of such programs may have had priorities other than scientifically sound cost-benefit evaluation or may have, in any case, done the best job possible considering available resources and other constraints.

and rigorously evaluated programs, a need we will take up in more detail in Chapter Four. That we have analyzed only two programs limits our ability to generalize the results; finding that these two programs save more than they cost obviously does not imply that dissimilar programs will do so. However, such a finding serves as proof of principle that programs generating a net savings do exist.

In this chapter, we first describe the criteria for selecting programs for this cost-savings analysis and show how the two programs selected meet the criteria (and how others do not). Then, we compare program costs to the government savings they generate in order to determine if public expenditure can be justified on the basis of a net savings to government. Finally, we additionally include some of the benefits to other individuals—those benefits that can be easily and incontrovertibly monetized. This leads us to a more comprehensive estimate of the monetary benefit to society of such programs than we get from our estimate of the benefits to the government alone. Even this more comprehensive estimate is still incomplete, however, since we are not able to monetize all of the benefits of the programs.

PROGRAMS SELECTED FOR ANALYSIS

As discussed in Chapter Two, while numerous early childhood intervention programs have been developed and tested, only a fraction of those have been evaluated in any fashion. Very few have been rigorously and thoroughly evaluated over long periods of time. Yet such an evaluation of the program is necessary for a defensible cost-savings analysis. Specifically, to implement our cost-savings analysis, we require that five criteria be met.

First, the evaluation must have an experimental design. It must measure the characteristics and behaviors of not only the treatment group but also a control group, i.e., a group comparable in all respects to the treatment group except that its members do not participate in the program. Should the groups then differ during or after the program in some measure of interest (e.g., time on welfare), that difference can be ascribed to the program. The ideal way to ensure an experimental design is to conduct a randomized trial. Subjects are assigned to the treatment group and the control group randomly. If the sample size is sufficiently large, this promotes the necessary similarity between the two groups.

There are other ways to evaluate program effectiveness. For exam-ple, one could measure the behavior of interest before the treatment and at some time thereafter. However, this type of evaluation is not applicable to an early childhood intervention program in which the subjects are developing children for whom the "before" value of the variable—time on welfare, in special education, etc.—is zero. One could also use a quasi-experimental design with retrospectively cho-sen control groups, although the inability to control for both ob-served and unobserved differences between treatment and control groups may bias such studies. While various statistical techniques are available to try to minimize these potential biases, we are not aware of any evaluations in the literature that employ these tech-niques and also meet our other criteria.

Second, the sample size must be large enough for true differences between the treatment and control groups to be recognizable with statistical methods. The larger the sample, the more likely that a measured difference of a certain size between the treatment and control groups will be judged statistically significant, i.e., the smaller the chance that the difference is a result of random variation. In practice, sample sizes are never large enough to totally eliminate the concern of sampling error, so we take the standard errors[6] of our savings estimates into account in drawing inferences from them.

Third, sample attrition over time must be small, for two reasons. First, attrition brings down the sample size. Second, differential at-trition can skew the results. For example, if many of the families with the lowest socioeconomic status do not complete the treatment or are not available for later follow-up, the treatment and control groups will not be adequately comparable.

Fourth, the program outcomes or potential benefits (such as reduc-tion in welfare usage) that lead to cost savings must be measured in the evaluation. For obvious logistical and budgetary reasons, the evaluator of a program can measure only a limited number of out-comes. In many of the program evaluations described in the litera-ture, outcomes that imply direct cost saving have not been mea-sured. Theoretically, the cost savings could be estimated on the basis

---

[6]The standard error, or standard deviation, is a measure of the degree to which a set of numbers vary from their mean.

of the outcomes that *have* been measured. But this can be done only if there is a well-understood relationship between the measured outcomes and the unmeasured, cost-saving outcomes (e.g., between juvenile arrest record and time in prison as an adult). The selection of outcomes for inclusion in the evaluation is often based on the theory behind the program. For example, a program designed to improve cognition may measure the child's IQ. The program may also reduce welfare usage later in the child's life, but if that particular outcome is not measured, the cost savings associated with reduced welfare usage probably cannot be calculated (because of the lack of a clear relationship between IQ and welfare usage).

Finally, and most important, long-term follow-up of the subjects is required if savings are to be fully accounted for. Most of the benefits that generate monetizable cost savings occur long after the intervention has been completed. Adequate time between the intervention and the measurement of outcomes must have elapsed for the benefits of interest to have occurred. An evaluation that follows subjects for only a few months or even years cannot be used to predict long-term benefits, and thus cost savings, with any confidence. In practice, evaluation periods have not been long enough to capture all the lifetime benefits to program participants, partly because early intervention experiments were not conducted before the 1960s. For a cost-savings analysis, either the unobserved future benefits must be estimated from outcomes that have been observed or some long-term benefits must be omitted from the calculation, leading to an underestimate of the savings associated with the program.

Of the programs we identified in the published literature, only two meet all these criteria. They are the Elmira PEIP and the Perry Preschool program. While most of the other programs we reviewed in Chapter Two meet the first three criteria (design, sample sizes, and attrition), they are more problematic in terms of the remaining two criteria. For example, only the Early Training Project, Chicago CPC, Carolina Abecedarian, and Syracuse FDRP have follow-ups that are as long as that of the Elmira PEIP (through age 14, 15, or 19), and no other program matches the age-27 follow-up available for Perry Preschool participants. At the same time, with the exception of measures of crime and delinquency in the CPC and FDRP programs, these programs largely did not assess measures of other outcomes for the child or mother that can be readily monetized (e.g., employment, welfare utilization). While these types of benefits may be measured in future follow-ups, any estimates of savings based on current information would be incomplete. Thus, we have chosen not to undertake cost-savings analyses for programs where estimates of savings would be highly uncertain or clearly underestimated. However, as we note below, for the two programs we do analyze, concerns about the precision and comprehensiveness of our estimates of savings still remain, although to a lesser degree than would be the case for the programs we did not consider.

Both the Elmira PEIP and Perry Preschool program are described in detail in Chapter Two. Below, we emphasize those aspects of program design that permit fulfillment of the criteria given above or that are otherwise particularly germane to the cost-savings analysis.

The Elmira PEIP

As described in Chapter Two, the Elmira PEIP home-visits program helped infants and their mothers by providing parent education, social support for the mother, and referrals to social services starting in the prenatal period and continuing until the child turned 2. The program services were delivered through home visits to first-time mothers by trained nurses. The program cost on the order of $6,000 (in 1996 dollars) per child. This paid for the average of 32 home visits that occurred during pregnancy and the first two years after birth.

The evaluation of the Elmira PEIP home-visits program was based on an experimental design, with mothers randomly assigned to treatment and control groups. Subjects in the program have been followed to age 15. Attrition over that period has been on the order of 20 percent for the children, less for the mothers.

For purposes of analyzing the long-term follow-up results of the Elmira PEIP, Olds et al. (1997) report results for the full experimental group, as well as a higher-risk subsample. This latter group consists of women who, at the time of enrollment in the study, were unmarried and had low socioeconomic status (SES). In the results we present below, we separately evaluate savings for this higher-risk sample, as well as for the remaining experimental sample, which we call lower-risk.[7] The lower-risk group thus consists of two-parent families or higher-SES families. At the time of the age-15 follow-up, there were 100 families in the higher-risk group (i.e., treatment plus control) and 145 families in the lower-risk group. These represent adequate sample sizes. However, they are small enough that we still have to be concerned with the uncertainty surrounding the estimates of effectiveness and thus of cost savings.

A follow-up through age 15 is long enough to capture many of the cost savings generated by the program. (Table 3.1 lists the outcomes measured by the Elmira PEIP evaluation and those we monetize.) However, 15 years is not long enough to derive estimates of the child's lifetime employment or welfare utilization. For instance, since 15-year-olds have little employment history, there are no good early indicators on which to base predictions of lifetime employment performance. In contrast, criminal careers can be predicted for the children on the basis of arrest records of 15-year-olds.

Our cost-savings analysis builds upon an earlier assessment of the Elmira PEIP, conducted with data measured for children and their mothers when the children were 4 (Olds et al., 1993). Two years after the program ended, the cost-savings analysis showed government savings that just exceeded program costs for low-income families (a net savings of $180 per child in 1980 dollars). For the sample as a whole, government savings did not exceed costs; rather savings to government provided only a partial offset to program costs. In both cases, the bulk of government savings resulted from reductions in the use of AFDC and other social welfare programs by the mother. The data available for our analysis of the children through age 15 permit an even more comprehensive assessment of longer-term savings generated by the program for both children and their mothers.

---

[7]As discussed in Chapter Two, at the time of the age-15 follow-up, the significant differences were primarily for the higher-risk families. We are grateful for the separate unpublished results for those in the lower-risk sample that were provided by David Olds.

Table 3.1

Outcomes Measured in Elmira PEIP

Domain	Mother/ Child	Outcome Description
Child development	Child	IQ at age 3 IQ at age 4
Parent development	Mother	Home environment at age 4 Reports of child abuse and neglect through age 15
Education	Mother	Years of education at age 4
Employment	Mother	*Months employed through age 15*
Welfare	Mother	*Months on AFDC through age 15* Months on Food Stamps through age 15 Months on Medicaid through age 15
Crime	Mother	*Arrests through age 15* Convictions through age 15 *Jail days through age 15*
	Child	*Arrests through age 15* Convictions through age 15
Health	Mother	Subsequent pregnancies and births through age 15 Months between 1st and 2nd birth through age 15 Substance abuse impairments through age 15
	Child	*ER visits, ages 25–50 months* Hospital days, ages 25–50 months

NOTES: Age references are to the age of the focal child. For annotated outcome tables, see Tables 2.2, 2.3, A.1, and A.3. Italics indicates benefits we monetized.

The Perry Preschool Program

The Perry Preschool program, also reviewed in Chapter Two, provided preschool classes to a sample of children in Ypsilanti, Michigan, when they were 3 and 4 years old. The program cost, measured in 1996 dollars and discounted to the birth of the participating child, were about $12,000 per child.[8] Program costs were associated with time spent in preschool (two and a half hours a day, five days a week,

---

[8]This is a weighted average that accounts for the fact that about 20 percent of participants attended only one year of the two-year program (Barnett, 1993).

for three-quarters of the year), as well as weekly (one and a half hour) home visits by the child's preschool teacher.

The Perry Preschool program evaluation is based on an experimental design with random assignment to treatment and control groups. The sample (treatment plus control) includes 123 children from 100 families. Subjects of the evaluation have been followed through age 27, with an attrition rate of about 9 percent. Again, the sample size is adequate to make estimates but not to eliminate substantial uncertainty surrounding the outcomes and the cost savings.

Evaluations of the Perry Preschool program provide estimates of the program results for participating children versus the control group in terms of education, employment and income, welfare, and crime (see Table 3.2 for the outcomes measured and those previously monetized by Barnett (1993) that are incorporated in our analysis). The long follow-up period, longer than that in the Elmira PEIP evaluation, permits estimates of welfare costs and taxes from increased employment that are generated during adulthood by children who participated in the program. In addition, Barnett (1993) provides estimates of projected savings, beyond age 27, as a result of higher taxes from employment, lower welfare utilization, and reduced crime.

Data from the Perry Preschool long-term follow-up have been previously used by Barnett (1993) to conduct a cost-benefit analysis based on data from the age-27 follow-up. Barnett's estimates, consistent with early cost-benefit assessments of the program, indicate that savings to government exceed program costs by a factor of more than 7 to 1. The largest component of savings is from reductions in crime, a large fraction of which is the estimated reductions in the intangible losses to victims of crime over the lifetime of the program participants. Other large savings components include taxes recovered over participants' lifetimes because of higher earnings, and reduced K–12 education costs.

In the analysis we report below, we have used Barnett's results to calculate savings, generated by the Perry Preschool program, from higher employment and reductions in the utilization of welfare, the

Table 3.2

Outcomes Measured in Perry Preschool

Domain	Mother/ Child	Outcome Description
Child development	Child	IQ at age 5
		IQ at age 7
		IQ at age 8
		IQ at age 14
Education	Child	Achievement test score at age 9
		Achievement test score at age 14
		High school GPA at age 19
		Time in special education through age 19
		Years in educable mentally impaired programs through age 27
		Years retained in grade through age 27
		High school graduation rate by age 27
		Postsecondary education credits by age 27
Employment	Child	*Employment rate at age 19*
		Employment rate at age 27
		Monthly earnings at age 27
Welfare	Child	*Received public assistance at age 27*
		Received public assistance in last 10 years at age 27
Crime	Child	*Ever arrested by age 27*
		Lifetime arrests through age 27
Health	Child	Teen pregnancies per 100 females through age 19

NOTES: Age references are to the age of the focal child. For annotated outcome tables, see Tables 2.2, 2.3, and B.1. Italics indicates benefits monetized by Barnett (1993) that we adjusted to 1996 dollars and rediscounted.

criminal justice system, and special education.[9] For comparability with our analysis of the Elmira PEIP, Barnett's figures have been adjusted to 1996 dollars and rediscounted.   On balance, these changes decrease estimates of both costs and savings. More important, our figures also differ from those reported in Barnett because we have elected, as discussed more fully below, not to monetize the reduction in pain and suffering for victims of crime. Thus, our esti-

---

[9]Barnett (1993) also includes savings to government from reduced use of adult education and the increased costs to government from greater participation in college. These two factors are small and nearly cancel each other out.

mates of the benefits to the rest of society are a more conservative figure than those reported by Barnett.

COMPARING PROGRAM COSTS TO THE GOVERNMENT SAVINGS THE PROGRAMS GENERATE

Early childhood intervention programs generate at least four types of significant savings to government:

- **Increased tax revenues.** These result from increased employment and earnings by program participants, including income tax at the federal and state levels, Social Security contributions by both the employer and employee, and state and local sales taxes. The Perry Preschool program measured the increased employment and income for the children in the evaluation through age 27, and Barnett (1993) projected future earnings and income through age 65. The employment and earnings measures in the Elmira PEIP are limited to gains experienced by the mother through age 15 of the child.

- **Decreased welfare outlays,** including Medicaid, Food Stamps, and AFDC, and general assistance (typically funded by counties). The savings to government include not only the reduced payments to recipients but also the reduced administrative expenses. The Perry Preschool evaluation took account of all of these factors, measuring welfare utilization effects for the children through age 27 and projecting future savings through age 65 based on Barnett's (1993) calculations. The Elmira PEIP measured changes in months spent on welfare by the mother (and child) through age 15 of the child.

- **Reduced expenditures for education, health, and other services.** Examples are special education, emergency room visits, and stays in homeless shelters. The Elmira PEIP evaluation measured emergency room visits when the child was between the ages of 25 and 50 months. The Perry Preschool program evaluation measured net education savings through when the child was in high school (i.e., savings due to lower special education expenditures and less grade repetition net of increased schooling costs due to greater educational attainment). To the extent that the programs reduce the need for other special services that were not measured in the evaluations, the savings figure is an under-estimate of the true savings to government.

- **Lower criminal justice system costs,** including arrest, adjudication, and incarceration expenses. On the basis of the measured outcomes, we can predict criminal activity and thus criminal justice expenditures for the lifetime of the subject; therefore, the estimate of criminal justice savings covers the entire lifetime of the children in the Elmira PEIP and Perry Preschool interventions. In addition, the criminal justice system savings for mothers in the Elmira PEIP are included based on treatment- versus control-group differences in arrests and jail days through when the focal child was 15.

Estimates of government savings in each of these categories can be derived from the outcome data collected in the evaluations of the two programs included in this analysis. (Note that some of the outcomes listed in Tables 3.1 and 3.2, e.g., increased IQ, may result in savings or costs to the government, but these are not easily quantified and are not included here.) In the results that follow, all dollar amounts are expressed in 1996 dollars. Net present values are estimated as of the birth of the child using a 4 percent discount rate.[10] The sensitivity of our results to the choice of the discount rate is addressed at the end of the chapter.

Elmira PEIP, Higher-Risk Families

Table 3.3 summarizes the costs and savings to government of the Elmira PEIP home-visit program for higher-risk families. These savings are estimated from benefits reported by Olds et al. (1994, 1997) and Olds (1996). The details of the calculations are outlined in Appendix A.

---

[10]By net present value, we mean the sum of the dollar amounts over all future years, discounted at a constant rate per year to take into account the fact that future dollars are worth less than today's dollars.

Table 3.3

Costs and Savings: Elmira PEIP, Higher-Risk Families

	Dollars per Child			
	Due to Mother	Due to Child	Total	SE
Program cost			6,083	
Savings to government	20,384	4,310	24,694	6,420
Reduction in health services	*	115	115	56
Taxes from increased employment	5,683	*	5,683	3,681
Reduction in welfare cost	14,067	*	14,067	4,905
Reduction in criminal justice cost	634	4,195	4,828	1,900
Net savings			18,611	

SOURCE: Authors' calculations. See Appendix A for additional detail.

NOTES: * = not measured. All amounts are in 1996 dollars and are the net present value of amounts over time where future values are discounted to the birth of the participating child, using a 4 percent annual real discount rate. The standard error (SE) of individual line items in this table was estimated by multiplying the SE of the item's cost driver times the cost factor that converts the cost driver into estimated cost. For example, for welfare the cost driver is months on welfare, and the cost factor is the cost per month. The SE of the cost driver is estimated as one-fourth of the 95 percent confidence interval estimate of the difference between the treatment- and control-group outcomes. The SEs of the totals were approximated by the square root of the sum of squared SEs of the components. These estimates of the SEs are very rough, but they are sufficiently accurate to convey the level of uncertainty in the estimated program benefits caused by the small sample size.

The difference between the total savings ($24,694)[11] and the cost ($6,083) is the net savings to government ($18,611). The overall amount of savings is over four times the cost of the program. So this program clearly pays for itself through the reductions it enables in future spending on existing government programs.

Over 80 percent ($20,384) of the savings we can estimate is due to differences between the treated group and the control with respect to behavior of the mother during the first 15 years of the child's life. In particular, mothers in the treated group were employed more and used welfare less. The rest of the savings are from differences in the

---

[11]We show all numbers to the nearest dollar, so that readers can follow our calculations without the impediment of rounding errors. Obviously, the level of precision shown is much greater than the data can support. Our conclusions do not depend on it.

child's behavior ($4,310), primarily due to less crime over his or her lifetime.[12]

The behavior of both the mother and the child has been observed for only 15 years. We have made no attempt to estimate the increases in the child's future income (and thus increases in tax revenue) or decreases in the child's use of welfare that may result from the child's participation in the program. Likewise, we have we not attempted to guess at the possible increases in employment (and thus income and tax revenue) nor decreases in welfare usage by the mother after the child is 15 years old. We have also not monetized other beneficial effects of the program through age 15 of the child, such as those from reduced child abuse and neglect. Thus, the calculated net savings ($18,221) is likely an underestimate of the true savings to government that can be credited to this program.

Figure 3.1 depicts the sources of government savings for the Elmira PEIP home-visit program for higher-risk families. Over half the savings to government result from reductions in welfare costs. The remainder is split evenly between increased tax revenues and decreased criminal justice costs.

Note that the program cost occurs at the time of the intervention, while the savings to government stretch out into the future. (In Table 3.3, the savings figure is a cumulative sum of those future savings, appropriately discounted.) In Figure 3.2 we show how those savings accumulate over time. The curves in the figure represent cumulative costs and savings through different years since the intervention, measured by the age of the child. Each point on a curve is the net present value (using a 4 percent discount rate) of the annual amounts up to that time. The home visits provided by the program stop after the child is 2 years old, so the cumulative cost curve levels off at two years.

---

[12]For convenience, we use average savings per child. For example, we do not mean to suggest that a typical child enrolled in the Elmira PEIP program would have cost the criminal justice system another $4,195 without the program. Many of these children incurred no criminal justice costs during their lifetimes. But some incurred very large expenses, resulting in the average $4,195 figure when those amounts are spread out over everyone.

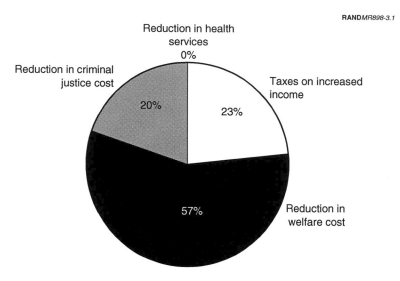

RAND*MR898-3.1*

SOURCE: Table 3.3 and authors' calculations.

**Figure 3.1—Sources of Savings to Government:
Elmira PEIP, Higher-Risk Families**

In contrast, the savings continue to accumulate long after the intervention is complete. We see that the cumulative savings exceed cumulative program costs after only three years. Many of the savings from this program start soon after the intervention because so many of the savings result from changed behavior of the mother. We emphasize here that the savings occur early because we will see that this is not true in the case of the Perry Preschool program.

Elmira PEIP, Lower-Risk Families

Table 3.4 summarizes costs and savings to government of the Elmira PEIP home-visits program for lower-risk families. Again, these savings are estimated from benefits reported by Olds et al. (1994, 1997) and Olds (1996). The details of the calculations are included in Appendix A.

We see that when this home-visits program serves families from the lower-risk group, there are no net savings to government—the total

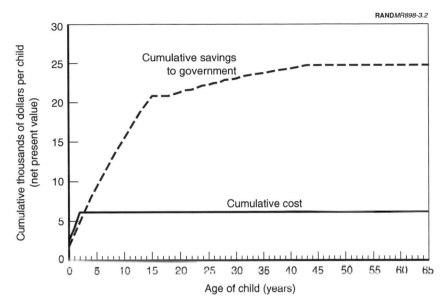

SOURCE: Authors' calculations. See Appendix A for additional detail.

**Figure 3.2—Cumulative Costs and Benefits: Elmira PEIP,
Higher-Risk Families**

savings to government do not exceed the program costs. Although mothers from families participating in the program have more employment (resulting in increased tax revenues) and less use of welfare than mothers from the control group, the differences are not large enough to generate sizable savings. Likewise, children receiving the intervention were less involved in criminal activity than those in the control groups, resulting in a savings to the government in criminal justice costs. However, those savings ($1,143) are much less than they are for the higher-risk families ($4,195).

It is important to keep in mind, however, that the program may generate future savings to government as the participants continue to age. As with the higher-risk families, any difference between treatment and control groups in terms of the future earnings and welfare utilization for children are not observed and therefore not included in the savings estimates.

Table 3.4

Costs and Savings: Elmira PEIP, Lower-Risk Families

| | Dollars per Child | | | |
	Due to Mother	Due to Child	Total	SE
Program cost			6,083	
Savings to government	2,525	1,250	3,775	5,591
Reduction in health services	*	107	107	47
Taxes from increased employment	1,144	*	1,144	3,101
Reduction in welfare cost	1,270	*	1,270	4,483
Reduction in criminal justice cost	111	1,143	1,254	1,246
Net savings			−2,307	

SOURCE: Authors' calculations. See Appendix A for additional detail.

NOTES: * = not measured. All amounts are in 1996 dollars and are the net present value of amounts over time where future values are discounted to the birth of the participating child, using a 4 percent annual real discount rate. The standard error (SE) of individual line items in this table was estimated by multiplying the SE of the item's cost driver times the cost factor that converts the cost driver into estimated cost. For example, for welfare the cost driver is months on welfare, and the cost factor is the cost per month. The SE of the cost driver is estimated as one-fourth of the 95 percent confidence interval estimate of the difference between the treatment- and control-group outcomes. The SEs of the totals were approximated by the square root of the sum of squared SEs of the components. These estimates of the SEs are very rough, but they are sufficiently accurate to convey the level of uncertainty in the estimated program benefits caused by the small sample size.

Since we do observe net savings when the program was offered to higher-risk families, we cannot blame the program design for the lack of savings for lower-risk families. Rather, it results from the choice of subjects. This is illustrated in Table 3.5, which considers just one category of savings, welfare usage by the mothers. Without the services of the home-visits program, the mothers' usage of welfare over the first 15 years of the child's life is considerably less for those from the lower-risk group than for those from the higher-risk group (30 and 90 months, respectively). As might be expected from Table 3.5, the home-visits program reduces welfare usage by mothers in the lower-risk families only slightly below the already (relatively) low level in the controls. However, the program reduces welfare usage by mothers in the higher-risk families by 33 percent. One way to interpret these results is that lower-risk families need less assistance of the type offered by the program, so the program cannot accomplish as much. This underscores the need for matching the program

Table 3.5

**Different Baselines May Explain
Different Improvements**

Recipients	Months Mother on Welfare During Child's First 15 Years	
	No Program	Home-Visits Program
Higher-risk families	90	60
Lower-risk families	30	28

SOURCE: Olds et al, 1997, and unpublished tabulations provided by David Olds.

to the population that needs its services; at least from the perspective of government savings, appropriate targeting is crucial.

Perry Preschool Program

Table 3.6 summarizes costs and savings to government of the Perry Preschool program. Our calculations are based on those reported in Barnett (1993), although they are updated to 1996 dollars and re-discounted to present value as of the birth of the participating child for comparability with other amounts reported here. As we note above, we have also omitted some of the factors included in the Barnett (1993) estimates. The details of the calculations are included in Appendix B.

The savings to government ($25,437) are over twice as large as the program costs ($12,148), yielding net savings to government of $13,289. So, like the Elmira PEIP home-visits program for higher-risk families, the Perry Preschool program pays for itself through future reductions in government expenditures.

The entries in the "mother" column of Table 3.6 are all unmeasured. It is not surprising that only the economic benefits to the child have been measured in the evaluation of this program, since it is a preschool program designed to improve child outcomes. Nonetheless, preschool is a form of child care, so conceivably some of the program mothers may have been able to increase their employment over what it would have been without the program (thus increasing

Table 3.6

Costs and Savings: Perry Preschool

	Dollars per Child			
	Due to Mother	Due to Child	Total	SE
Program cost			12,148	
Savings to government	*	25,437	25,437	5,789
Reduction in education services	*	6,365	6,365	51
Taxes from increased employment	*	6,566	6,566	3,319
Reduction in welfare cost	*	2,310	2,310	4,422
Reduction in criminal justice cost	*	10,195	10,195	1,713
Net savings			13,289	

SOURCE: Authors' calculations. See Appendix B for additional detail.

NOTES: * = not measured. All amounts are in 1996 dollars and are the net present value of amounts over time where future values are discounted to the birth of the participating child, using a 4 percent annual real discount rate. The standard error (SE) of individual line items in this table was estimated by multiplying the SE of the corresponding line item in Table 3.3 by the square root of the inverse ratio of sample sizes. The assumption is that the population variability for each item in the Perry Preschool sample is the same as in the Elmira PEIP higher-risk sample, so only sample size makes the standard errors of mean values differ. This assumption makes the estimated standard errors in this table even rougher than those in Table 3.3. However, they are still sufficiently accurate to convey the uncertainty of estimated program benefits.

income and tax contributions and decreasing welfare consumption). To the extent that the program enables mothers to work more, the calculated net savings is an underestimate of the true savings to government that can be credited to this program.

Figure 3.3 shows how the savings to government are distributed among the four savings categories. Forty percent of the savings to government are from reductions in criminal justice system costs, because treated children commit less crime as they transition through adolescence to adulthood. Greater tax revenues as a result of greater employment and income over the lifetime of the child accounts for 26 percent of the savings. Lower use of education services—such as special education participation—accounts for another 25 percent of the savings. Reduction in the child's lifetime usage of welfare accounts for the remaining 9 percent of the savings to government.

In Figure 3.4 we show how the costs and government savings of the Perry Preschool program accumulate over time. As in Figure 3.2, the curves in this figure represent cumulative costs and savings through

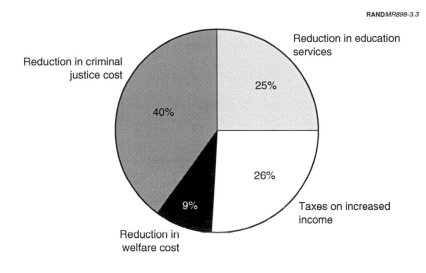

SOURCE: Table 3.6 and authors' calculations.

Figure 3.3—Sources of Savings to Government: Perry Preschool

different years since the intervention, measured by the age of the child. The preschooling provided by the program occurs when the child is 3 and 4 years old, so the cumulative cost curve is zero until three years and levels off at four years. As was true with the Elmira PEIP home-visits program, the savings continue to accumulate long after the intervention is complete, but in the case of the Perry Preschool program the cumulative savings do not exceed program costs for 21 years. There are two reasons for this. First, the cost per participant in the Perry Preschool program is higher than the cost per family in the Elmira PEIP home-visits program (roughly, $12,000 versus $6,000). Second, in contrast to the Elmira PEIP, all the measured benefits of the Perry Preschool program accrue to the child, and most of the government savings arising from those benefits to the child do not occur until the child transitions through adolescence to adulthood.

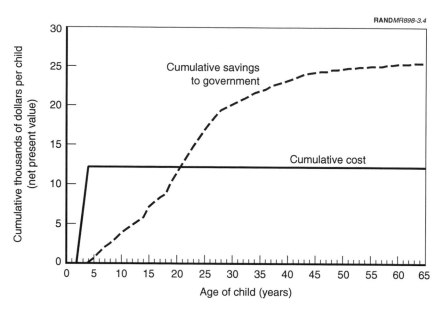

SOURCE: Authors' calculations. See Appendix B for additional detail.

Figure 3.4—Cumulative Costs and Benefits: Perry Preschool

Summary

Figure 3.5 summarizes the results of our cost-savings analysis. The black bars represent the program costs. The gray bars represent the total savings to government. The difference between the bars is the net savings. As we have already seen, both the Elmira PEIP home-visits program for higher-risk families and the Perry Preschool program generate more than enough savings to offset program costs. However, when the participants of the Elmira PEIP home-visits program are from lower-risk families, the savings do not offset the costs.

Note that the uncertainty caused by the small sample sizes must be considered. The error bars on the savings estimates represent 66 percent confidence intervals, meaning that the true value of the savings has a two-thirds chance of being in the interval, a one-sixth chance of being above the interval, and a one-sixth chance of being

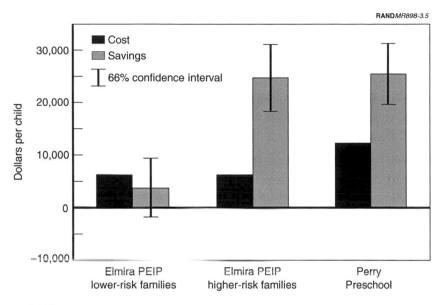

SOURCE: Tables 3.3, 3.4, and 3.6.

NOTE: All amounts are in 1996 dollars and are the net present value of amounts over time where future values are discounted to the birth of the participating child, using a 4 percent annual real discount rate.

Figure 3.5—Program Cost Versus Savings to Government

below the interval. Doubling the size of these intervals would give a 95 percent confidence interval. These error bars are very wide and suggest caution in ascribing a particular savings number to these programs. We can be much more confident, as far as statistical uncertainty goes, in asserting that the savings associated with the Elmira PEIP when offered to higher-risk families are greater than the costs of that program. The same goes for the savings and costs associated with the Perry Preschool program. However, in the case of the savings associated with the Elmira PEIP when offered to lower-risk families, the confidence interval dwarfs our "best estimate" of small possible savings. Thus, these savings may well be positive but, if so, are small, and in all likelihood do not compensate for the program's costs.

The error bars in Figure 3.5, however, capture only statistical uncertainty—that associated with possible divergence from "true" values (those obtained with very large populations) when the number of subjects is not very large. Recall that the estimates of net savings to government are also subject to uncertainty because some of the benefits to project participants have not been included in the cost-savings analysis. Most important, employment and welfare benefits to the child as well as long-term employment and welfare benefits (i.e., those beyond 15 years) to the mother are not included in the Elmira PEIP analyses; no employment and welfare benefits to the mother (regardless of timing) are included in the Perry Preschool analysis. Moreover, additional benefits to the programs may have been experienced by program participants but not measured by the evaluations of those programs.

Another source of uncertainty limits the inferences that can be drawn from these results. For various reasons, scaling up these small demonstrations into broadly implemented programs could result in changes in benefits (probably reductions) and costs. The magnitude of these changes is unpredictable. Scale-up problems are discussed in more detail in the next chapter.

Although Figure 3.5 implies different net savings for the Elmira PEIP and Perry Preschool program, it is not appropriate to compare the two savings figures to decide which of the two programs is better. This is because the outcomes measured by the program evaluations—and thus the types of savings included in our analysis—differ between the two programs.

ADDITIONAL MONETARY BENEFITS TO THE REST OF SOCIETY

As discussed at the beginning of this chapter, the savings to government represents only part of the monetary benefit to society as a whole. Society benefits from early childhood interventions in other ways as well. Two such benefits are

- the greater income enjoyed by program participants than by comparable persons who did not participate[13]

- the savings to persons who, in the absence of the program, would have been crime victims.[14]

The increase in income for program participants is calculated straightforwardly from data already given above. It is the amount by which increases in participants' employment income exceeds reductions in the welfare they receive. Benefits to those who would have been crime victims, or losses to real crime victims, are not so straightforwardly calculated.

Crime victim losses can be divided into two categories: tangible and intangible losses. Tangible losses to the victim include property loss, medical expenses, and the income lost while injured. Intangible losses refer to pain and suffering. Tangible losses are relatively easy to estimate because the estimates can be based upon empirical evidence. On the other hand, experts disagree about how to count intangible losses. One way is to assume that the average jury award to a crime victim in compensation for pain and suffering represents the value of those intangible losses. Another way is to assume that what people are willing to pay to avert those losses represents their value. (What they are willing to pay could be measured by what they pay for crime protection devices like burglar alarms, for example, or by what they say they would pay when they respond to carefully constructed surveys.)

These two different ways of monetizing the intangible crime losses lead to very different figures. In our analysis, we avoid this contro-

---

[13]We began this chapter by searching for benefits from early interventions beyond the families they were intended to serve. While increased income to participants is not in direct terms such a benefit, these persons *are* part of society at large, and increased production benefits everyone indirectly. The amount of the benefit may not be equal to the income. In fact, a program participant, rather than occupying a new job slot, may be displacing someone else from an existing slot, so there may be no change in economic activity (and there may also be none of the new taxes counted above as benefits). However, full credit is typically taken for such increases in personal income in social-welfare analyses, and we follow suit here.

[14]The reasoning here is that, as shown above, early interventions discourage criminal careers. Implementing such programs thus reduces the losses to society from crime.

versy by omitting the intangible losses from our calculations.[15]   To the extent that the value of the intangible losses is great, our estimate of savings to persons who would have been crime victims is conservative.

Table 3.7 and Figure 3.6 show the results of adding these two sources of savings to the savings given in the preceding tables. In all three cases, more fully accounting for societal benefits naturally makes the programs look even better. In the case of the higher-risk families in the Elmira PEIP home-visits program, the more complete estimate of monetary benefit to society exceeds the estimate of savings to government alone by about 25 percent. Most of the additional benefit to society comes from the savings to crime victims. The gain in participant income is small because the gain in employment income is largely (although not completely) offset by the loss of welfare income. In the case of the Perry Preschool program, including these additional monetary benefits nearly doubles our previous estimate. In the case of the lower-risk families in the Elmira PEIP home-visits program, the positive savings to crime victims and additional participant income add to the small savings to government associated with this program. The savings to government and additional monetary benefits just exceed program costs.

It is important to note that these crime-related and participant income benefits are not the only other monetary benefits to society generated by early childhood intervention programs. Thus, the totals in Table 3.7 and Figure 3.6 are not a full estimate of the monetary benefits to society.

SENSITIVITY OF RESULTS TO DISCOUNT RATE

All monetary figures in this analysis are given as the sum of the dollar amounts over all future years, but discounted to present value (as of the birth of the participating child). This takes into account the assumption common to much economic analysis that future dollars

---

[15]Note that our approach differs from Barnett (1993) who includes intangible losses from crime in his estimates of the benefits of the Perry Preschool program.

Table 3.7

Benefits to Society from Analyzed Early Intervention Programs
(dollars per child)

	Elmira PEIP		Perry Preschool
	Lower-Risk	Higher-Risk	
Savings to government	3,775	24,694	25,437
Additional monetary benefits	2,938	6,072	24,535
Increase in mother's income net of welfare loss	1,622	1,010	NA
Increase in child's income net of welfare loss	NA	NA	13,846
Reduction in tangible losses to crime victims	1,315	5,062	10,690
Savings plus additional monetary benefits	6,713	30,766	49,972

SOURCE: Authors' calculations. See Appendixes A and B for additional detail.

NOTES: NA = not applicable. All amounts are in 1996 dollars and are the net present value of amounts over time where future values are discounted to the birth of the participating child, using a 4 percent annual real discount rate.

are worth less to people than today's dollars, quite apart from the effects of inflation. Choice of discount rate is the subject of considerable debate among economists. The 4 percent used here falls within the range of rates commonly used in public-policy analysis and is consistent with previous RAND cost-effectiveness analyses.[16]

Because the benefits are spread over so many years after the intervention, the estimated net present value of the benefits is very sensitive to the choice of discount rate. Even small variations (say, 1 percentage point above or below our base-case rate) affect the estimates appreciably. Figures 3.7 and 3.8 show how the choice of discount rate affects our estimates of government savings and monetary benefit to society for the Elmira PEIP higher-risk sample and the Perry Preschool sample, respectively. Despite the sensitivity to the discount rate, both the Elmira PEIP for the higher-risk sample and the Perry Preschool program generate positive savings to government and to society as a whole for a reasonable range of rates.

_____

[16]This is a real discount rate, i.e., one that ignores inflation or, to put it another way, that applies after the effects of inflation have been taken into account.

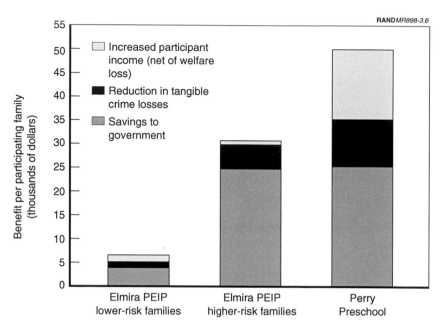

SOURCE: Table 3.7.

NOTE: All amounts are in 1996 dollars and are the net present value of amounts over time where future values are discounted to the birth of the participating child, using a 4 percent annual real discount rate.

Figure 3.6—Benefits to Society from Elmira PEIP and Perry Preschool

FINDINGS FROM COST-SAVINGS AND COST-BENEFIT ANALYSES

In our cost-savings analysis, we analyzed two early childhood intervention programs—one that involves home visits from prenatally to when the child is 2 and focuses upon the mother, and one that involves preschool for children who are 3 and 4 years old. We have seen that these two very different programs can generate significant savings to government that exceed their costs. This supports

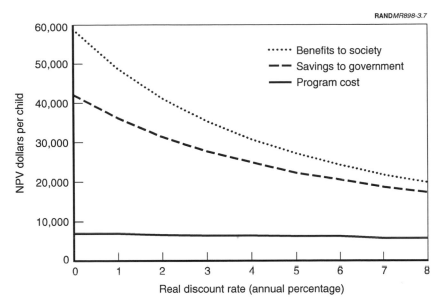

SOURCE: Authors' calculations. See Appendix A for additional detail.

Figure 3.7—Sensitivity of Estimated Cost and Benefits to Discount Rate: Elmira PEIP, Higher-Risk Families

the argument that public funding of such programs may be justified.[17] Other programs like these two, or other types of programs, may also generate savings to government, but none has the evaluation characteristics needed to estimate long-term cost savings with any accuracy. Although the two programs we have evaluated vary in their net savings, we cannot conclude that one type of program is better than the other, because the cost-savings numbers are not directly comparable (as a result of differences in the outcomes monetized).

---

[17]Before it can be said that funding any given program is justified on the basis of a cost-savings (or cost-benefit) analysis, other uses of the money with potentially more favorable cost-savings ratios must be taken into account, along with other public priorities and budgetary constraints.

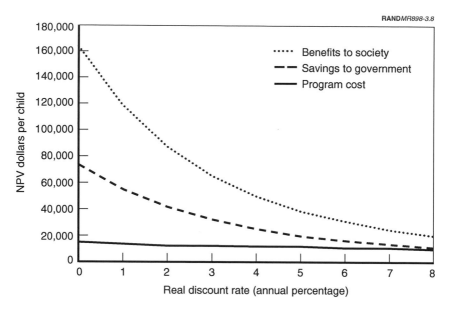

RANDMR898-3.8

SOURCE: Authors' calculations. See Appendix B for additional detail.

**Figure 3.8—Sensitivity of Estimated Cost and Benefits to Discount Rate:
Perry Preschool**

Our analysis shows that, while costs accrue at the time of program participation, the savings to government take a considerable amount of time, at least a few decades, to accumulate. The home-visits program appears to generate savings earlier than does the preschool program, which means the payback period is likely to be much shorter. In other words, one program might be considered a shorter-term investment than the other. This may, however, be an artifact of the Perry Preschool evaluation's not attempting to measure any benefits for parents. Among the benefits we monetize in our analysis, those attributable to changes in parents' behavior generate savings sooner than benefits attributable to the child, most of which do not pay off until the child is grown. In any event, because the purpose of these programs is to promote child development, not to earn quick savings for the government, the payback period should not be used to decide between programs that offer different benefits to the child.

We see from comparing the net savings from the Elmira PEIP offered to higher-risk families (which were substantial) to those from the same program offered to lower-risk families (which were negative) that targeting matters. In other words, if program participation is not limited to the neediest families, net savings to government may not be generated.

Finally, we see that the monetary benefit to society—even the partial estimate provided here—is even larger than the savings to government alone. This is because there are persons who, in the absence of the program, would have been victimized by crime and who, if the program is implemented, are not. These persons experience a significant monetary benefit in forgone medical expenses and property losses. Also, children in the Perry Preschool program, by age 27, experience a monetary benefit related to the increase in their income. Likewise, mothers participating in the Elmira PEIP demonstrated an increase in their earned income. However, in the case of the Elmira PEIP home-visits program, the net income gains to the mother are small because the increase in employment income is largely offset by a decrease in welfare income. In addition, in considering any income-related findings from the Elmira PEIP, it must be kept in mind that participating children have not aged sufficiently to determine any income effects for them.

Chapter Four

ISSUES RELEVANT TO INVESTMENT DECISIONS

This chapter summarizes the findings of the previous chapters and outlines their implications for future research and for policy. So far, we have shown that early intervention programs can improve childhood development and maternal well-being and may generate future savings that more than offset their costs. While these results are encouraging for policymakers considering future investments in targeted early intervention programs, they are based on a limited number of mostly smaller-scale demonstration programs implemented up to three decades ago. These limitations raise the following issues, which remain to be addressed:

- The optimal design of programs in terms of the services they provide and the developmental stage at which intervention occurs.

- The ways in which programs can best be targeted to those children and families who will benefit most.

- The replicability of findings from smaller-scale studies to full-scale implementation of model programs.

- Recognition of the full range of benefits yielded, including those outside the original program objectives.

- The implications of the changing social safety net.

In the following pages, we discuss these issues, concluding with potential roles for policymakers at different levels of government who are exploring further investments in early childhood programs.

WHAT WE KNOW ABOUT EARLY CHILDHOOD INTERVENTION

Early intervention programs are not designed to a single standard. This report has documented that early childhood intervention programs display a range of characteristics, depending on the objectives of each particular program. Programs differ in terms of which members of the family they target, the risk factors used to select participants, the segment of childhood during which the intervention takes place, and the services offered as part of the treatment.

Despite the diversity of design, most programs share the same underlying assumption: Early childhood—the prenatal period through the beginning of school—is a unique developmental period that serves as a foundation for behavior, well-being, and success later in life. Some children are subjected to stressors during early childhood that impede normal development. These stressors may include insufficient cognitive stimulation, nutritional deprivation, inadequate health care, and maladaptive social interaction. Early intervention to correct these impediments has the potential to promote healthy development in at-risk children.

Numerous studies have documented a range of potential benefits of early intervention for children and their families. These benefits span the domains of cognitive and behavioral outcomes, educational attainment, economic resources, and health. Our cost-savings analysis and the work of others (Barnett, 1993) have shown that these benefits have the potential to generate savings to government that more than pay for the cost of the program generating them. However, one of the most important findings of this report is that programs do not always generate savings to offset their costs. What seems to make a difference in terms of whether a program generates savings to government?

- *Targeting.* Programs that target children and families who will benefit most from the services offered have the highest chance of repaying their costs. In most cases, more disadvantaged children are likely to realize the greatest benefits. In some cases, however, children who face the greatest number of risks may require even more specialized services, so they may benefit less from a particular program than children who face only a few risks.

- *The time horizon required for the payback of program costs.* In contrast to program costs, which accrue during the course of the program, most program savings are not realized for years, accumulating over the life of the child and mother. The longer the time period permitted for the payback, the greater the chance that the savings generated by program benefits will outweigh the program's costs.

- *The evaluation's inclusion or exclusion of outcome measures for the mother* (typically determined by whether the program's objectives include improving the mother's effectiveness or well-being). One of the findings of this report is that while early childhood programs are generally designed to improve children's well-being and achievement, many of the programs also influence mothers' outcomes. Improvements in mothers' outcomes may generate savings to government that are as large or larger than the savings generated by improvements in the children's outcomes. In addition, savings arising from changes in mothers' outcomes often accrue immediately as well as in the future.

In sum, early intervention programs show promise in their potential for helping program participants and having positive spillover effects for other members of society:

- For high-risk children, early intervention may lower the chance that they will become chronic or violent criminals or fall behind in schoolwork, and may raise the likelihood that they achieve economic self-sufficiency.

- For high-risk mothers, these programs may improve their quality of life not only by improving their children's well-being and achievement, but also by giving them such benefits as increased employment, reduced drug dependency, and more.[1]

---

[1]It might have been anticipated that programs such as nurse home visits would improve parenting and child outcomes at the expense of maternal employment and income. Instead, higher-risk families in the Elmira PEIP exhibited improvements in maternal income *and* in child outcome measures.

- For individual states and communities, early intervention pro-grams may be a means of reducing the escalating costs of cor-rections, welfare, and special education.

- For the economy as a whole, early intervention may be a way to improve overall social welfare, while reducing the pain and suf-fering associated with criminal victimization.

These benefits, together with the savings realized from some of these programs, raise the question, Why aren't we spending more as a na-tion on early intervention?   Currently, the bulk of public-sector spending on children occurs during the school-age years (Haveman and Wolfe, 1995).   For example, in 1992, about 8 percent of the total public investment in the average child was spent during the first five years—the first quarter—of childhood.   That amounted to about $1,500 per year per child (in 1992 dollars) and included expenditures for early childhood development, welfare, and health care.   For chil-dren age 6 to 18, public spending averaged approximately $6,500 per child per year (in 1992 dollars).   The difference was due primarily to expenditures on primary and secondary schools.   Other public ex-penditures for children those ages include funds for criminal justice, youth employment, and other youth programs.

We do not know to what extent, if any, a greater balance should be sought between these two amounts. Why not? First, because even interventions with exemplary designs and evaluations have been marked by methodological irregularities or constraints, leaving some room for uncertainty about the validity of their findings. Second, be-cause, methodology aside, there are still many important aspects of these programs about which we know relatively little. The next segment of this chapter enumerates these factors and discusses why they are important. The final segment discusses further steps in early intervention research and evaluation that could help resolve some of the unknowns and determine whether broad funding of these promising programs is justified.

WHAT WE DON'T KNOW ABOUT EARLY CHILDHOOD INTERVENTION

The two most important things we don't know about early childhood intervention programs is why the successful programs work—and why those not shown to be successful don't. If we knew which aspects of program design and clientele targeting influenced program success, it would be possible to make educated judgments about the likelihood of a program's success. Under the current state of knowledge, however, such predictions cannot be made with certainty, and any new proposal would have to be tested and evaluated if it is to be regarded as promising. The first two unknowns discussed below are elaborations on this theme. The final three are other important issues yet to be answered.

Are There Optimal Program Designs?

There are many aspects of program design that early intervention researchers would like to learn more about. Some of the unanswered questions regarding design are fundamental and relate to the macro-level design features of the program. These include the following:

- Can better results be achieved by treating both the child and the mother rather than by focusing on only one?

- At what point in early childhood is it best to intervene—infancy or preschool? Or, is it better to intervene continuously throughout the entire period of early childhood?

- Would programs combining interventions (e.g., training for parents and classroom experience for children) yield greater, fewer, or the same benefits as those expected from the sum of the individual interventions?

- Does the intensity of the program make a difference, such as the frequency of home visits or the number of hours spent in center-based care?

- What are the implications of the quality of the services provided, including the background, training, and supervision of day-care providers, educators, or those making home visits, and the resources used in the program (e.g., staff to child ratios, curriculum, educational materials)?

- Should the intervention be the same for each child, or should it vary with the special needs of each child?

Although these issues remain largely unexplored, the programs we reviewed in Chapter Two provide some insight. For example, the evaluation of the Chicago CPC suggests that the duration of time spent on preschool and school-age interventions does matter. Likewise, the experimental design features of the Abecedarian and Project CARE programs demonstrate the effectiveness for some outcomes of combining preschool and after-school interventions, and the advantage of combining home visits and center-based day care. Based on findings from the IHDP, more-intensive participation in intervention services appears to generate more-favorable effects. A comparison across programs suggests that programs targeting both parent and child may be most effective. Other child care research has shown that more provider training appears to yield greater benefits for children, but it is not clear how much more provider training is optimal or what type is needed (Roupp et al., 1979; Whitebook et al., 1989). While these findings are suggestive, they provide only limited guidance for designing optimal programs.

Unanswered questions regarding program design must be faced not only by individuals responsible for implementing early intervention programs but also by government policymakers deciding whether to fund them. For example, it is popular to tailor programs to meet the needs of specific communities, such as offering bilingual preschool in Hispanic communities. It is unclear how to balance the advantages of tailoring program designs to community needs against the potential disadvantages of deviating from standardized program designs that strive to achieve optimal training, intensity, and curriculum.

How Can Programs Best Be Targeted to Those Who Will Benefit Most?

As discussed in numerous places in this report, one of the unifying concepts of the early intervention programs we surveyed was the idea that the beneficiaries of treatment would be children who were at risk. By "at risk" we mean children who were subjected to one or more stressors in the form of cognitive, emotional, or resource deficiencies. A number of studies document larger gains for subjects who are at lower levels of socioeconomic or developmental status (e.g., see the review in Barnett, 1995; and Olds et al., 1997), although the presence of many risk factors may actually make it difficult to improve outcomes through standard intervention programs (Liaw and Brooks-Gunn, 1994). The importance of targeting is verified by our study of the differences in cost-savings from the Elmira PEIP delivered to a "higher-risk" sample and a "lower-risk" sample. Our analysis shows that while the savings generated by the program through children's age 15 more than offset the costs for the higher-risk group, the program does not generate nearly as much savings for the lower-risk group. Despite these and other findings, whether and how to target are still controversial issues (Liaw and Brooks-Gunn, 1994; Ramey and Ramey, 1994; Reynolds et al., 1997).

Targeting thus remains an imprecise concept, and knowledge regarding the merits of alternative definitions of risk is scant. For instance, it is unknown whether the children who would benefit most from early intervention are best identified on the basis of biological, cognitive, emotional, or resource risk factors (or some combination thereof). Children who face multiple risks may require even more specialized interventions than those that are effective for children who experience one or only a few risks. Furthermore, children may be exposed to varying levels of different types of risk over the course of their lives, raising the possibility that the optimal targeting strategy might fluctuate with age, or that risk might compound over time. The possible linkages and interactions between programs that target at-risk children early in life and those that intervene later on are other issues that deserve further attention.

The choice of risk criterion may be influenced by the total number of children who meet it—a number that has obvious budgetary implications. Data limitations preclude a careful assessment of the exact number of young children who might be deemed "at risk" based on various measures of socioeconomic, cognitive, or biological factors. To provide a rough guide to the number of children that might be targeted using socioeconomic criteria, we tabulated data from the March 1996 Current Population Survey (CPS), a nationally representative sample of approximately 60,000 civilian households. Demographic characteristics, household structure, and annual family income information reported in the CPS can be used to identify young children in households with the following three risk factors: single-mother family, mother less than age 19 at birth of child, and family income less than 200 percent (or 150 percent or 100 percent) of the poverty line.[2] Similar criteria were used, for instance, to select mothers and children for participation in the Elmira PEIP.

Based on data for the cohort born in the year prior to the March 1996 CPS interview, Table 4.1 reports the estimated number of children born each year with any one of the three risk factors, first for all children and then for first-born children (another selection criteria used in the Elmira PEIP). Of the approximately 3.3 million births identified in the CPS that year, between 3 and 43 percent (113,000 to 1.4 million) would meet one of the risk factors listed in the table. The largest fraction are born into families with annual income less than 200 percent of the poverty line. That percentage is reduced by half when the income cutoff is 100 percent of the poverty line. Over 1 in 7 children is born to a single mother. A much smaller share, about 3

Table 4.1

Number and Percentage of Children Born with Various Risk Factors

				Risk Factor		
		Single-Mother	Mother Less Than	Family Income Less Than x Percent of the Poverty Line		
	Total	Family	Age 19	$x = 200$	$x = 150$	$x = 100$
All children						
N (1,000s)	3,277	482	113	1,418	1,083	737
Percentage	100.0	14.7	3.4	43.3	33.0	22.5
First-born children						
N (1,000s)	1,166	129	52	363	256	172
Percentage	100.0	11.1	4.5	31.1	22.0	14.8

SOURCE: Authors' tabulations using March 1996 Current Population Survey.
NOTE: Weighted count of children age less than 1 in families with reported characteristics as of March 1996.

---

[2]We show results for three income levels relative to the poverty line because program targeting criteria may not be limited to those who are defined as officially poor using the current government definition. For example, in the IHDP, at-risk children were defined based on biological risk; while this was correlated with poverty, only about half the families had income less than 150 percent of the poverty line. In recognition of the limits of the current poverty standard for identifying disadvantaged families, some targeted, even means-tested, programs are using multiples of the poverty line. For example, many of the state Medicaid expansions include families with incomes up to 185, 200, 225, and even 300 percent of the poverty line.

percent, are born to a teenage mother. About 35 percent of all children are born to first-time mothers. (Within this group, the percentages in most risk categories are lower than that for all mothers, since first-time mothers are less likely to be single parents or poor.)

When risk factors are considered together (using a poverty cutoff of 150 percent), the tabulations reveal that 36 percent of all children born (1.2 million) are subject to at least one of the three risk factors, and just under 14 percent (451,000) are subject to two or more risk factors. Only a small fraction, 1.3 percent, are subject to all three risk factors.

Keeping in mind that these data are only intended to provide rough approximations, it is clear that a substantial number of children might be targeted for early intervention, at least based on socioeconomic criteria. For example, the selection criteria used in the Elmira PEIP would target upwards of 25 to 30 percent of all children born to first-time mothers. If the same criteria were applied to all newborns, an even larger percentage—approximately three times the absolute number of children— would be affected. If the results of the Elmira PEIP were replicated on a larger scale, the benefits measured in that model program might accrue to a large number of the nation's children.

Can Model Programs Be Replicated on a Large Scale?

One of the key unknowns regarding widespread government administration of early intervention programs is what is referred to as the "scale-up" issue (Gomby et al., 1995). With the exception of Head Start and the Chicago Child-Parent Centers, the programs reviewed in Chapter Two are small-scale model programs, implemented in a specific community by researchers with expertise in child development. The concern here is that early childhood programs administered by public agencies in a diverse array of communities will not replicate the model programs researchers studied, for several reasons:

- It is unclear whether public agencies would garner enough resources to adequately duplicate the model programs. Recent public sentiment indicates fiscal conservatism (see Hosek and Levine, 1996) mixed with a reluctance to eliminate public spending on current programs oriented toward children (see Reynolds et al., 1997).

- Public programs would be unlikely to attract staff with the same training and stake in the outcomes as the staff who implemented the research programs. For example, the Perry Preschool staff were certified to teach in elementary, early childhood, and special education, and they participated in ongoing supervisory and training activities. In contrast, teachers in the Head Start program have historically had considerably lower levels of training, although recent efforts have aimed to improve teacher quality (Zigler and Styfco, 1993; Zigler, Kagan, and Hall, 1996).

- Programs administered by government on a large scale would have to deal with issues that the model programs did not face, such as how to ensure consistency across many program sites and how to screen large numbers of children. Also, as "free" resources, they would face demands for inclusion by lower-risk individuals and groups whose children could cost the same to serve but benefit less than those for whom the program was originally intended.

In the end, the expansion or replication of a given early intervention model may dilute some program benefits, while others may remain equally strong.

Our primary example of large-scale national implementation of a program modeled after an experimental program is Head Start, and this example highlights the importance of the issues just enumerated. At its inception in the 1960s, Head Start enjoyed great public support. In contrast, in recent budgetary recommendations the Congressional Budget Office recommended eliminating Head Start (CBO, 1997). What accounts for this turnabout are research findings that Head Start does not meet its expectations regarding improvements in IQ scores and academic achievement. Best publicized are findings that the cognitive gains achieved by Head Start children fade after only a few years of elementary school (see, for example, McKey et al., 1985). Even the favorable findings of the Perry Preschool project across a variety of outcome measures failed to mollify Head Start's critics, who pointed out the difficulty of replicating such demonstration projects. For example, CBO (1997) writes: "Some early intervention efforts have provided evidence of long-term improvement in the lives of participants, but those projects were much more intensive—and expensive—than Head Start" (p. 166). At the same time, the limitations of many of the Head Start evaluations, highlighted in Chapter Two, cast doubt on firm conclusions about the program's benefits or lack of benefits.

While the research community recognizes the issue of large-scale replication as an important unanswered question, few examples other than the Head Start experience provide much insight into the issue.[3] One effort currently under way, which may contribute greatly to understanding scale-up issues for one of the model programs reviewed in Chapter Two, is being conducted by the University of Colorado's Center for the Study of Prevention of Violence. This initiative, known as "Blueprints," will assist communities in replicating the Elmira PEIP home-visits program and others across multiple sites (Pentz, Mihalic, and Grotpeter, 1997; McGill, Mihalic, and Grotpeter, 1997). In addition, with support from the Department of Justice, issues of larger-scale implementation are being studied for the PEIP model through new programs implemented in six low-income neighborhoods in cities in California, Florida, Missouri, and Oklahoma.

What Benefits Do Programs Generate Beyond Their Objectives?

This report has stressed that there is not one accepted model of early childhood intervention but rather that programs vary in their design features: the criteria used to target children and families, the services provided, the child's age at which treatment occurs, the type and level of treatment for parents, and a number of other dimensions. The features of a program typically reflect its objectives. For in-

---

[3]Several of the two-generation programs reviewed in St. Pierre, Layzer, and Barnes (1995) and IRP (1997b) have been implemented on a large scale, although in several cases they are not replicating a proven model program. Results based on experimental evaluations of these programs for short-term effects (through age 5) are mixed. It is difficult to assess whether the absence of strong beneficial effects (consistent with those of the model programs we review in Chapter Two) is because of the program design, implementation, or quality of the evaluation. In most cases, the two-generation programs deliver less-intensive services for children, compared in particular with such model programs as the IHDP and the Carolina Abecedarian, which may explain the absence of even short-term cognitive effects for the children.

stance, programs like the Perry Preschool (which emphasized preparing children for school) may select children based on cognitive and socioeconomic criteria, may choose preschool as the primary treatment, and may involve the parent little. On the other hand, programs that focus on improving child health and development might choose a different slate of design features. An example of the latter type is the Elmira PEIP, which selected participants on the basis of socioeconomic status only, used nurse home visits as the principle treatment, and interacted primarily with the parent rather than the child.

Results from both of the interventions highlighted in our cost-savings analysis indicate, however, that a program may generate benefits beyond the compass of its objectives. For example, the Perry Preschool not only fulfilled the objectives many people might associate with preschool—developmental and short-term educational benefits—it also yielded long-term educational, economic, crime prevention, and health-related benefits. Program evaluations, however, do not always account for these extended benefits. The Abecedarian project emphasized improving cognition and education and only measured those outcomes. But the results of the Perry program, which also provided intensive child care, suggest that the Abecedarian children would have been likely to exhibit other improvements.

If program designers recognize that benefits may exceed objectives, they would be more likely to monitor a range of outcomes beyond their focus. This would enrich our understanding of the relationship between program design and outcomes.

What Are the Implications of the Changing Social Safety Net?

All of the early intervention benefits we have highlighted may depend upon the other private and public resources that form the social safety net. The recent federal welfare reform act (the 1996 Personal Responsibility and Work Opportunity Reconciliation Act) and associated state and local reform efforts may dramatically change the environments of children most at risk, along with the resources available to them. The nature of these effects is currently uncertain, so the implications for the costs and savings presented in this report are unpredictable. We highlight two possible implications here.

First, many of the model intervention programs we evaluated integrated their services with other components of the social safety net. For example, in Elmira, New York, one of the components of the PEIP was to link program participants with social services for which they qualified. Other programs, too, increased participants' awareness of other public-sector programs that they could participate in. Thus, the magnitudes of the effects of the interventions may be due to both the services provided by the program and the linkage to other publicly provided social services. If those services were not available, the measured benefits of the intervention may be different. To the extent that the intervention and other social service programs are complementary, the magnitude of the intervention effects would most likely be smaller. Alternatively, to be most effective in the post–welfare reform environment, early intervention programs may need to incorporate new services and features to compensate for aspects of the social safety net that have been altered. These new program components would most likely increase costs and further alter the cost-savings equation.

Second, to the extent that expenditures on welfare by all levels of government decline, the savings that early intervention generates by reducing welfare costs will also decline. The effect on savings generated in other cost categories is unclear. Again, our understanding of this issue depends upon further study of intervention programs under the new welfare regime. For the present, it may be helpful to qualitatively review some of the possible outcomes of the legislation:

- Some mothers previously on AFDC will get jobs and improve their socioeconomic status. This may have the effect of turning some "higher-risk" families into "lower-risk" families. That, in turn, may decrease the number of families likely to provide a return to the government on an early intervention investment. Whether it does will depend partly on the quality of day care received by the children of these newly working mothers. If that care is better than what they might receive as part of an intervention, the savings to government from early intervention for some population groups will probably drop and possibly disappear.

- Some mothers previously on AFDC will not get jobs, but their loss of welfare income from higher levels of government (i.e., the federal level) will largely be compensated by lower levels (i.e., state and local governments). For such mothers in the "higher-risk" category, the savings to government from returns on early investment may not change much, depending on the specifics of implementing state or local welfare benefits.

- Some mothers previously on AFDC will not get jobs and will not see their federal aid replaced in any meaningful way by state or local governments. Children of such families could become even greater burdens to government in terms of future special-services and criminal justice costs than they are now. Their future earning power could also decrease, and with it the taxes they pay. The government could thus realize even greater savings in attempting through early intervention to avert such costs. It is uncertain whether the increase in those savings would offset the decrease in welfare-related savings resulting from the welfare cutback.

At this time, we cannot predict the portion of currently high-risk families that will fall into each of these categories. The implications for the benefits associated with any of the model early intervention programs reviewed in Chapter Two and the associated cost-savings analysis conducted in Chapter Three are thus unknown.

A related issue concerns the social and economic changes that have transformed the opportunities and challenges faced by today's families with young children. What do these changes imply for the costs and benefits of early intervention programs? Most of the targeted early intervention programs reviewed in Chapter Two were conducted in the 1960s and 1970s. While this has permitted long-term follow-up of the participants' outcomes, the magnitude of the effects of these programs measured for earlier cohorts may differ for today's counterparts. It is difficult to infer whether the effects of similar programs implemented today would be larger or smaller.

Each of these concerns suggests that there is further uncertainty over the exact magnitudes of the benefits that will be generated by future early intervention programs, and the cost-savings estimates associated with those programs. This uncertainty points, even more strongly, toward the need for ongoing evaluations of early intervention programs involving more recent cohorts of children and their families.

NEXT STEPS FOR RESEARCH AND POLICY

Clearly, more research is needed to address the unanswered questions surrounding early childhood intervention programs. As federal, state, and local entities proceed to implement early childhood intervention programs, it is essential that these efforts be accompanied by careful, well-designed evaluation studies so that we continue to learn about which investments have the greatest payoff. While the expansion of existing programs and the initiation of new programs appear to be proceeding on a decentralized basis, our understanding of how these programs work and what their benefits are will be enhanced through a more centralized, coordinated, and comprehensive research program.

New demonstrations are needed to answer questions that require variations in program design or that reflect the evolving society and economy, and broader testing of previous designs is required to answer questions of scale-up and replicability of program benefits for diverse communities and other at-risk populations. However, on questions of targeting, benefits beyond objectives, and other issues, much could also be gained—and less expensively—by making the most of evaluations already under way. This could include several strategies:

- *Continuing to follow participants in existing samples* so that follow-up periods are long enough to measure such long-term implications as high school graduation, welfare participation, and adult earnings. For example, the Consortium for Longitudinal Studies pooled original data from 11 intervention programs in the 1960s (including the Early Training Project and the Perry Preschool discussed in Chapter Two) and then, in 1976, conducted a collaborative follow-up of the original subjects (Lazar and Darlington, 1982).

- *Expanding the range of outcomes measured in ongoing evaluations* so that a comprehensive understanding of the potential benefits of alternative interventions could be developed. For instance, rather than simply measuring IQ and special education placement, child care interventions could also monitor health and behavior. Other interventions that focus on parents as well as children could measure short-run and long-run outcomes for both.

- *Making more effort to collect measures that are comparable to those of other studies* so that better comparisons could be made across intervention strategies, targeting criteria, or other variations in program designs.

In addition, researchers need to continue to develop and employ appropriate statistical and econometric techniques that allow evaluation of quasi-experimental or nonexperimental designs. It may not always be possible or desirable to implement randomized control trials when evaluating new, possibly larger-scale, intervention programs. Ethical concerns or resource constraints may pose barriers to implementing the number of randomized control trials necessary to investigate the range of design questions that need to be answered. However, as demonstrated by the recent evaluations of Head Start and the Chicago Child-Parent Centers discussed in Chapter Two, reasonable inferences can be drawn about program effects using state-of-the-art methodologies to account for nonrandom program participation, yielding important insights that can help guide program development and implementation. These strategies may be useful for evaluating many of the larger-scale programs already under way, or those that will soon begin in communities across the country.

Any effort to fund new and expanded demonstrations and enhance data collection from ongoing evaluations would benefit from a strong federal role. Despite the changes in welfare funding, the federal government still stands to benefit greatly from early intervention through increases in income and Social Security tax revenues and decreases in federal public assistance and criminal justice system spending. In addition, the federal government, through its broader jurisdiction, has greater potential to coordinate, if not fund, an integrated program of research and development in early childhood intervention. The federal role could encompass establishing standards for program evaluation, encouraging the implementation of multiple site programs, and disseminating the results of diverse program efforts.

State governments also stand to gain by playing a leading role in further development of early intervention programs. State legislators should find in early intervention programs an additional option for addressing crime, welfare, and special education needs that may cost less than the current approaches and be less punitive and stigmatizing than other options. Governors and their staffs have the opportunity to take the lead in sponsoring model programs—and in ensuring that responsible evaluation accompanies innovative programs. Though a given state would be unlikely to invest in the array of programs that the federal government could test, the accumulation of experience across a variety of state models would be useful to all concerned.

While federal and state agencies could provide funding and expertise as to what works and what doesn't, designers of particular demonstrations may also benefit from the knowledge and expertise of community-based organizations and local agencies in adapting their programs to local needs. Such organizations could also provide an existing structure for recruiting and training staff and conducting community outreach, and could provide support for rigorous evaluation. Community-based organizations would presumably welcome these programs, not only for their child development benefits but also as another tool in building an integrated strategy to achieve various community aims including, for example, violence prevention and poverty reduction. And local agencies principally interested in issues other than child development would appreciate the potential spillover benefits from early intervention—for example, in the quality of life and financial independence of young mothers.

While all efforts should be made to pursue low-cost, high-payoff strategies across all levels of the public sector, the nation should not shrink from major research investments in demonstrations, evaluations, and other activities that will address the issues we raise in this chapter. These activities will require a substantial commitment of funds—most likely in the millions or even the tens of millions of dollars. However, the early intervention programs that may prove warranted, and that some people are already advocating, will represent a national investment in the hundreds of millions or billions of dollars. A modest if substantial expenditure initiated now could thus ensure that maximum benefits are achieved from a much larger expenditure over the long term.

To put the need for a continuing research program in perspective, it is worth noting that in areas such as health, energy, and transportation, about 2 to 3 percent of total expenditures are devoted to research and development (R&D) efforts that improve the efficiency and effectiveness of spending in those areas. In contrast, recent estimates indicate that less than four-tenths of one percent of total federal government expenditures on children and youth in the United States goes toward R&D—about $2 billion out of $500 billion in fiscal year 1995 (National Science and Technology Council, 1997).[4] Including private sector spending almost certainly lowers the share of total spending on children that is devoted to R&D.

Given the gap between the share of expenditures devoted to R&D for children compared with the share for other areas of major national concern, we are almost certainly underinvesting in R&D related to children. As new initiatives lead to increased spending on the period of early childhood, it is essential that a comprehensive, sustained, and coordinated R&D program accompany those efforts. By adding to our understanding of which programs work and why, we can help ensure that investments made in the nation's children produce the highest possible benefits.

---

[4]This estimate corresponds with our information about R&D spending in the Head Start program: In fiscal year 1996, an estimated one-third of one percent of the federal expenditure for Head Start went toward R&D (Reynolds et al., 1997).

CALCULATION OF THE COSTS AND BENEFITS OF THE ELMIRA PRENATAL/EARLY INFANCY PROJECT

In this appendix, we discuss in detail the calculation of costs and benefits of the Elmira PEIP. (See Chapters Two and Three for more information about the Elmira PEIP.) David Olds and his colleagues compared costs and savings based on outcomes measured when the children were 4 years old (Olds et al., 1993). This analysis, which builds upon that work, incorporates outcomes measured when the children were 15 years old.

Different outcomes were observed, and thus different savings calculated, for higher-risk families and lower-risk families. The higher-risk subsample consists of families in which the mother, at the time of enrollment in the study, was unmarried and had a low SES. The lower-risk subsample consists of families with two parents or with higher SES. (See Chapter Three for more information about the subsamples.) Outcomes and savings for the higher-risk families are addressed in Tables A.1 and A.2; outcomes and savings for the lower-risk families are addressed in Tables A.3 and A.4.

As discussed in Chapter Three, savings to government that can be estimated on the basis of outcomes measured by the Elmira PEIP include employment effects; welfare effects; health services, which for the Elmira PEIP refers to child hospital emergency room visits; and crime effects. Table A.1 lists the outcomes measured in each of these four categories that are incorporated into the calculation of savings for higher-risk families. Note that not all of the outcomes measured by the PEIP evaluation, nor all of the outcomes measured that could conceivably lead to government savings, are included (see Table 3.1).

For example, although the number and timing of subsequent births have been measured, and reducing or delaying subsequent births could lead to government savings, we have not included these outcomes in our analysis (except to the extent that changes in fertility affect employment and welfare.)[1] The average outcomes per participant in both the experimental (E) and control (C) groups for the higher-risk families are tabulated in Table A.1.

The calculations that lead to the cost and savings numbers in Table 3.3 and the additional monetized benefit numbers in the PEIP higher-risk column of Table 3.7 are detailed in Table A.2. Program cost per participant is addressed in panel 1 of Table A.2. The government savings and additional monetized benefits, which are derived from the outcomes tabulated in Table A.1, are addressed in the rest of Table A.2 (panels 2–10). In each case, the dollar estimate reported is the average savings per participant. Dollar values are converted to 1996 dollars (using the Consumer Price Index (CPI)) and then converted to net present value (NPV) as of the birth of the participating child, using a 4 percent (real) discount rate.

The amount saved because of increased employment taxes is the difference between the treatment and control groups in months the mother is employed, multiplied by an estimate of the taxes generated per month (see panel 3). Savings due to decreased welfare usage (by the mother) and reduced special services (i.e., emergency room visits by the child) are each the difference in average outcome between the treatment and control groups multiplied by an estimate of the cost of that outcome (see panels 4 and 2, respectively). Assumptions behind the value estimates (i.e., tax or cost estimates) are chosen to match similar assumptions in the cost-benefit analysis of the Perry program by Barnett (1993). Savings due to decreased arrests and time in jail of the mother and decreased arrests of the child are also the difference in average outcome between the treatment and control groups multiplied by an estimate of the cost of the outcome (see panels 5 and 6, respectively).

---

[1]The number of days hospitalized was also measured (Olds, Henderson, and Kitzman, 1994). For the higher-risk families, the treatment average (0.65) was higher than the control average (0.13), but this results from one extreme case of illness that was unrelated to the quality of caregiving.

We also estimate the amount saved because of decreased future criminal involvement of the child (see panel 7). The criminal justice cost of an average adult criminal career is $27,350, in 1993 dollars, NPV at age 19, using a 4 percent discount rate (Greenwood et al., 1996, Table B.15, p. 57). The percentage of the population targeted by this intervention expected to have a criminal career (in the absence of the intervention) is assumed to be 66 percent. This is the same as assumed for the low-income welfare population targeted by the educational incentives program discussed in Greenwood et al., 1996 (Table B.1, p. 48). For the higher-risk families, the treatment reduces arrests through age 15 by 51.9 percent. Assuming that the decrease in adult criminal activity is 80 percent of this amount, the savings in criminal justice costs for adult criminal careers is ($27,350)(0.66)(0.519)(0.80) = $7,495 (in 1993 dollars, NPV at age 19, using a 4 percent discount rate).

The additional monetary benefits (mother's additional income from increased employment—less reductions in welfare payments—and decreases in tangible losses to crime victims) are derived from the government savings calculations (see panels 8–10).

Table A.3 lists, for the lower-risk families, the outcomes measured in each of the four categories that are incorporated into the calculation of savings (the same as in Table A.1) and tabulates the average outcomes for the experimental and control groups. The differences between the treatment and control outcomes for lower-risk families are typically smaller than the differences observed for the higher-risk families, recorded in Table A.1.

The calculations that lead to the cost and savings numbers in Table 3.4, and the additional monetized benefit numbers in the PEIP lower-risk column of Table 3.7, are detailed in Table A.4. Program cost per participant is addressed in the first part of Table A.4 (see panel 1). The government savings and additional monetized benefits, which are derived from the outcomes tabulated in Table A.3, are addressed in the rest of Table A.4 (see panels 2–10). As in Table A.2, in each case the dollar estimate reported is the average savings per participant, which are then converted to 1996 dollars and to net present value as of the birth of the participating child, using a 4 percent discount rate. The calculations parallel those in Table A.2.

Table A.1

Program Effects: Elmira PEIP, Higher-Risk Families

Type of Outcome	Who Is Observed?	Age of Child at Time of Observation	Outcome (Mean) Experimental Group	Control Group	Treatment Effect (E − C)	Effect Statistically Significant at .05 Level	Source
Health effects							
ER visits, ages 25 to 50 months	Child	4	1.18	1.72	−0.54	Yes	(1) p. 94
Employment effects							
Months employed through age 15	Mother	15	95.9	80.0	15.9	No	(2) p. 641
Welfare effects							
Months on AFDC through age 15	Mother	15	60.4	90.3	−29.9	Yes	(2) p. 641
Crime effects							
Arrests through age 15	Mother	15	0.18	0.58	−0.40	Yes	(2) p. 642
Jail days through age 15	Mother	15	0.04	1.11	−1.07	Yes	(2) p. 642
Arrests through age 15	Child	15	0.25	0.52	−0.27	Yes	(3)

NOTES: Age references are to the age of the focal child. E = experimental; C = control.

SOURCES: (1) Olds et al. (1994). (2) Olds et al. (1997). (3) Olds (1996).

Table A.2

Detailed Cost and Benefits: Elmira PEIP, Higher-Risk Families

Item	Estimate	Year $	NPV at Age	Discount Rate (%)	Source/Comments
1. Cost of Home Visits, Child Ages 0 to 2					
Cost per participant	$3,246	1980	0	3	Olds et al., 1993, p. 163
In 1996 $	$6,200	1996	0	3	1996 CPI/1980 CPI = 1.910
NPV with 4% discount rate	$6,033	1996	0	4	
2. Reduction in ER Visits by the Child, Child Ages 2 to 4					
Reduction in number of ER visits per child	0.54		NA	None	Table A.1
Cost per ER visit	$250	1996	NA	None	
Decrease in ER costs per child	$135	1996	NA	None	Reduction in ER visits * cost/visit
NPV at age 0	$115	1996	0	4	
3. Increase in Taxes from Mother's Increased Employment Income, Child Ages 0 to 15					
Increase in months employed per mother	15.9		NA	None	Table A.1
Monthly pay	$1,213	1991	NA	None	See Note (a)
Tax rate	0.35		NA	None	See Note (b)
Taxes paid per month	$425	1991	NA	None	Monthly pay * tax rate
Increase in taxes paid per mother	$6,750	1991	NA	None	Increase months employed * taxes/month
In 1996 $	$7,803	1996	NA	None	1996 CPI/1991 CPI = 1.156
NPV at age 0	$5,683	1996	0	4	

Table A.2—continued

Item	Estimate	Year $	NPV at Age	Discount Rate (%)	Source/Comments
4. Decrease in Cost to Government of Welfare Payments to Mother, Child Ages 0 to 15					
Reduction in months on welfare per mother	29.9				Table A.1
Monthly welfare payment	$553	1994	NA	None	See Note (c)
Ratio of welfare costs to welfare payments	1.1				See Note (d)
Cost per month of welfare	$608	1994	NA	None	Welfare payment * costs/payments ratio
Decrease in welfare costs per mother	$18,188	1994	NA	None	Decrease months on welfare * cost/month
In 1996 $	$19,316	1996	NA	None	1996 CPI/1994 CPI = 1.062
NPV at age 0	$14,067	1996	0	4	
5. Decrease in Mother's Arrest and Jail Costs, Child Ages 0 to 15					
Reduction in arrests per mother	0.40				Table A.1
Cost per arrest	$1,924	1993	NA	None	See Note (e)
Decrease in mother's arrest costs per mother	$770	1993	NA	None	Reduction in arrests * cost/arrest
Reduction in jail days per mother	1.07				Table A.1
Cost per day in jail	$27	1993	NA	None	See Note (f)
Decrease in mother's jail costs per mother	$29	1993	NA	None	Reduction in jail days * cost/day
Decrease in mother's arrest and jail costs per mother	$799	1993	NA	None	Decr. in arrest costs + decr. in jail costs
In 1996 $	$870	1996	NA	None	1996 CPI/1993 CPI = 1.089
NPV at age 0	$634	1996	0	4	
6. Decrease in Child's Arrest Costs, Child Ages 12 to 15					
Reduction in arrests per child	0.27				Table A.1
Cost per arrest	$1,924	1993	NA	None	See Note (e)
Decrease in child's arrest costs per child	$519	1993	NA	None	Reduction in arrests * cost/arrest
In 1996 $	$566	1996	NA	None	1996 CPI/1993 CPI = 1.089
NPV at age 0	$321	1996	0	4	

Table A.2—continued

Item	Estimate	Year $	NPV at Age	Discount Rate (%)	Source/Comments
7. Decrease in Criminal Justice System (CJS) Cost of Child's Adult Criminal Career, Child Ages 19 to 44					
CJS cost of adult criminal career	$27,350	1993	19	4	See Note (g)
% of target population having a criminal career	0.66				See Note (h)
CJS cost/control group child	$18,051	1993	19	4	CJS cost/career * percent w/ career
% reduction in arrests per child	0.519				Table A.1. 0.27/0.52=0.519
Fraction of adult criminal careers reduced	0.8				
Decrease in CJS costs of child's adult criminal career per child	$7,495	1993	19	4	See Note (i)
In 1996 $	$8,162	1996	19	4	1996 CPI/1993 CPI = 1.089
NPV at age 0	$3,874	1996	0	4	
8. Income from Mother's Increased Employment, Child Ages 0 to 15					
Increase in taxes paid per mother	$5,683	1996	0	4	Table A.2, panel 3
Ratio of income to taxes	2.428				See Note (j)
Increased employment income per mother	$13,798	1996	0	4	Increase in taxes * income/taxes
9. Decrease in Welfare Payments to Mother, Child Ages 0 to 15					
Decrease in welfare costs per mother	$14,067	1996	0	4	Table A.2, panel 4
Ratio of welfare cost to welfare payments	1.1				Table A.2, panel 4
Decreased welfare payments per mother	$12,788	1996	0	4	Decrease in costs / (costs/payments ratio)
10. Decrease in Tangible Losses to Crime Victims, Child Ages 19 to 44					
Decrease in mother's arrest and jail costs per mother	$634	1996	0	4	Table A.2, panel 5
Decrease in child's arrest costs per child	$321	1996	0	4	Table A.2, panel 6
Decrease in CJS costs of child's adult criminal career per child	$3,874	1996	0	4	Table A.2, panel 7
Ratio of tangible losses to CJS costs	1.0485				See Note (k)
Decreased tangible crime losses	$5,062	1996	0	4	See Note (l)

Table A.2—continued

NOTES: NA = not applicable (undiscounted); NPV = net present value; CPI = Consumer Price Index.

(a) The monthly pay estimate is the monthly equivalent of the $7 per hour (in 1991$) earned in 1989 by women who had been on AFDC in 1979–1981 (Nightingale and Haveman, 1995, p. 79).

(b) Taxes paid by the employee, across all levels of government, including Social Security taxes, are assumed to be 25% of the salary. Taxes paid directly by the employer, primarily the employer's contribution to Social Security, are assumed to be 10% of the salary. So the total additional taxes received by the government is 35% of the salary. These assumptions match those used in the analysis of the Perry Preschool program (Barnett, 1993, p. 504).

(c) The components of the $553 estimate are $378 for AFDC, $71 for Food Stamps, and $104 for Medicaid (all in 1994 $) (U.S. Bureau of the Census, 1996, Tables 597 and 602).

(d) It is assumed that welfare administrative costs are 10% of welfare payments, which is the same assumption made in the analysis of the Perry Preschool program (Barnett, 1993, p. 505). Thus the ratio of welfare costs to welfare payments is 1.10.

(e) Police cost per arrest is estimated to be $624, and adjudication cost per arrest is estimated to be $1,300; so total cost per arrest is $1,924 (1993 $) (Greenwood et al., 1994, Table 3.1, p. 15).

(f) Jail operating costs are estimated to be $10,000 per year (Greenwood et al., 1994, Table 3.1, p. 15). This corresponds to $27.40/day.

(g) These CJS costs include costs for arrest, adjudication, jail, and prison (Greenwood et al., 1996, Table B.15, p. 57).

(h) 66% is the same as for the low-income welfare population in the control group for the graduation incentives program discussed in Greenwood et al., 1996 (Table B.7, p. 51 and Table B.1, p. 48).

(i) CJS cost/control group participant * percent reduction in arrests * fraction of adult criminal careers reduced.

(j) Employment income, in these accounts, includes after-tax income plus fringe benefits. Assuming a marginal tax rate of 25% (for all types of taxes, including Social Security), after-tax income is 75% of salary, and assuming a 10% fringe benefit rate, total income is 85% of salary. Again, these are the same assumptions as are made for the analysis of the Perry Preschool program (Barnett, 1993, p. 504). Taxes are 35% of additional salary (see Note b above), so income is (85%/35%) = 2.428 times the taxes.

(k) In a typical criminal career, total estimated costs inflicted on victims is 4.5 times the CJS costs incurred (Schweinhart, 1993, p. 162). However, only 23.3% of the victim costs are tangible (Miller et al., 1996, p. 17). So, the ratio of tangible losses to CJS costs is (4.5)(0.233) = 1.0485.

(l) (Decrease in mother's arrest and jail costs + decrease in child's arrest costs + decrease in CJS costs of child's adult criminal career) * ratio of tangible losses to CJS costs.

Table A.3

Program Effects: Elmira PEIP, Lower-Risk Families

Type of Outcome	Who Is Observed?	Age of Child at Time of Observation	Outcome (Mean) Experimental Group	Control Group	Treatment Effect (E − C)	Effect Statistically Significant at .05 Level	Source
Health effects							
ER visits, ages 25 to 50 months	Child	4	0.89	1.39	−0.50	Yes	(1) p. 94
Employment effects							
Months employed through age 15	Mother	15	98.1	94.9	3.2	No	(2)
Welfare effects							
Months on AFDC through age 15	Mother	15	27.7	30.4	−2.7	No	(2)
Crime effects							
Arrests through age 15	Mother	15	0.10	0.14	−0.04	No	(2)
Jail days through age 15	Mother	15	0.00	2.32	−2.32	No	(2)
Arrests through age 15	Child	15	0.16	0.27	−0.11	No	(2)

NOTES: Age references are to the age of the focal child. E = experimental; C = control.

SOURCES: (1) Olds et al. (1994). (2) David Olds, April 3, 1997, personal communication.

Table A.4

Detailed Cost and Benefits: Elmira PEIP, Lower-Risk Families

Item	Estimate	Year $	NPV at Age	Discount Rate (%)	Source/Comments
1. Cost of Home Visits, Child Ages 0 to 2					
Cost per participant	$3,246	1980	0	3	Olds et al., 1993, p. 163
In 1996 $	$6,200	1996	0	3	1996 CPI/1980 CPI = 1.910
NPV with 4% discount rate	$6,083	1996	0	4	
2. Reduction in ER Visits by the Child, Ages 2 to 4					
Reduction in number of ER visits per child	0.50			None	Table A.3
Cost per ER visit	$250	1996	NA	None	
Decrease in ER costs per child	$125	1996	NA	None	Reduction in ER visits * cost/visit
NPV at age 0	$107	1996	0	4	
3. Increase in Taxes from Mother's Increased Employment Income, Child Ages 0 to 15					
Increase in months employed per mother	3.2		NA	None	Table A.3
Monthly pay	$1,213	1991	NA	None	See Note (a)
Tax rate	0.35				See Note (b)
Taxes paid per month	$425	1991	NA	None	Monthly pay * tax rate
Increase in taxes paid per mother	$1,359	1991	NA	None	Increase months employed * taxes/month
In 1996 $	$1,570	1996	NA	None	1996 CPI/1991 CPI = 1.156
NPV at age 0	$1,144	1996	0	4	

Table A.4—continued

Item	Estimate	Year $	NPV at Age	Discount Rate (%)	Source/Comments
4. Decrease in Cost to Government of Welfare Payments to Mother, Child Ages 0 to 15					
Reduction in months on welfare per mother	2.7		NA	None	Table A.3
Monthly welfare payment	$553	1994	NA	None	See Note (c)
Ratio of welfare costs to welfare payments	1.1				See Note (d)
Cost per month of welfare	$608	1994	NA	None	Welfare payment * costs/payments ratio
Decrease in welfare costs per mother	$1,342	1994	NA	None	Decrease months on welfare * cost/month
In 1996 $	$1,744	1996	NA	None	1996 CPI/1994 CPI = 1.062
NPV at age 0	$1,271	1996	0	4	
5. Decrease in Mother's Arrest and Jail Costs, Child Ages 0 to 15					
Reduction in arrests per mother	0.04		NA	None	Table A.3
Cost per arrest	$1,324	1993	NA	None	See Note (e)
Decrease in mother's arrest costs per mother	$77	1993	NA	None	Reduction in arrests * cost/arrest
Reduction in jail days per mother	2.32				Table A.1
Cost per day in jail	$27	1993	NA	None	See Note (f)
Decrease in mother's jail costs per mother	$64	1993	NA	None	Reduction in jail days * cost/day
Decrease in mother's arrest and jail costs per mother	$141	1993	NA	None	Decr. in arrest costs + decr. in jail costs
In 1996 $	$153	1996	NA	None	1996 CPI/1993 CPI = 1.089
NPV at age 0	$111	1996	0	4	
6. Decrease in Child's Arrest Costs, Child Ages 12 to 15					
Reduction in arrests per child	0.1		NA	None	Table A.3
Cost per arrest	$1,924	1993	NA	None	See Note (e)
Decrease in child's arrest costs per child	$212	1993	NA	None	Reduction in arrests * cost/arrest
In 1996 $	$230	1996	NA	None	1996 CPI/1993 CPI = 1.089
NPV at age 0	$157	1996	0	4	

Table A.4—continued

Item	Estimate	Year $	NPV at Age	Discount Rate (%)	Source/Comments
7. Decrease in CJS Cost of Child's Adult Criminal Career, Child Ages 19 to 44					
CJS cost of adult criminal career	$27,350	1993	19	4	See Note (g)
Percent of target population having a criminal career	0.22				See Note (h)
CJS cost/control group participant	$6,017	1993	19	4	CJS cost/career * percent w/ career
Percent reduction in arrests per child	0.407				Table A.3. 0.11/0.27=0.407
Fraction of adult criminal careers reduced	0.8				
Decrease in CJS costs of child's adult criminal career per child	$1,959	1993	19	4	See Note (i)
In 1996 $	$2,133	1996	19	4	1996 CPI/1993 CPI = 1.089
NPV at age 0	$1,012	1996	0	4	
8. Income from Mother's Increased Employment, Child Ages 0 to 15					
Increase in taxes paid per mother	$1,144	1996	0	4	Table A.4, panel 3
Ratio of income to taxes	2.428				See Note (j)
Increased employment income per mother	$2,777	1996	0	4	Increase in taxes * income/taxes
9. Decrease in Welfare Payments to Mother, Child Ages 0 to 15					
Decrease in welfare costs per mother	$1,270	1996	0	4	Table A.4, panel 4
Ratio of welfare cost to welfare payments	1.1				Table A.4, panel 4
Decreased welfare payments per mother	$1,155	1996	0	4	Decrease in costs / (costs/payments ratio)
10. Decrease in Tangible Losses to Crime Victims, Child Ages 19 to 44					
Decrease in mother's arrest and jail costs per mother	$111	1996	0	4	Table A.4, panel 5
Decrease in child's arrest costs per child	$131	1996	0	4	Table A.4, panel 6
Decrease in CJS costs of child's adult criminal career per child	$1,012	1996	0	4	Table A.4, panel 7
Ratio of tangible losses to CJS costs	1.0485				See Note (k)
Decreased tangible crime losses	$1,315	1996	0	4	See Note (l)

Table A.4—continued

NOTES: NA = not applicable (undiscounted); NPV = net present value; CPI = Consumer Price Index.

(a) The monthly pay estimate is the monthly equivalent of the $7 per hour (in 1991$) earned in 1989 by women who had been on AFDC in 1979–1981 (Nightingale and Haveman, 1995, p. 79).

(b) Taxes paid by the employee, across all levels of government, including Social Security taxes, are assumed to be 25% of the salary. Taxes paid directly by the employer, primarily the employer's contribution to Social Security, are assumed to be 10% of the salary. So the total additional taxes received by the government is 35% of the salary. These assumptions match those used in the analysis of the Perry Preschool program (Barnett, 1993, p. 504).

(c) The components of the $553 estimate are $378 for AFDC, $71 for Food Stamps, and $104 for Medicaid (all in 1994 $) (U.S. Bureau of the Census, 1996, Tables 597 and 602).

(d) It is assumed that welfare administrative costs are 10% of welfare payments, which is the same assumption made in the analysis of the Perry Preschool program (Barnett, 1993, p. 505). Thus the ratio of welfare costs to welfare payments is 1.10.

(e) Police cost per arrest is estimated to be $624, and adjudication cost per arrest is estimated to be $1,300; so total cost per arrest is $1,924 (1993 $) (Greenwood et al., 1994, Table 3.1, p. 15).

(f) Jail operating costs are estimated to be $10,000 per year (Greenwood et al., 1994, Table 3.1, p. 15). This corresponds to $27.40/day.

(g) These CJS costs include costs for arrest, adjudication, jail, and prison (Greenwood et al., 1996, Table B.15, p. 57).

(h) 22% is the same as for the general population (Greenwood et al., 1996, Table B.7, p. 51, and Table B.1, p. 48).

(i) CJS cost/control group participant * percent reduction in arrests * fraction of adult criminal careers reduced.

(j) Employment income, in these accounts, includes after-tax income plus fringe benefits. Assuming a marginal tax rate of 25% (for all types of taxes, including Social Security), after-tax income is 75% of salary, and assuming a 10% fringe benefit rate, total income is 85% of salary. Again, these are the same assumptions as are made for the analysis of the Perry Preschool program (Barnett, 1993, p. 504). Taxes are 35% of additional salary (see Note b above), so income is (85%/35%) = 2.428 times the taxes.

(k) In a typical criminal career, total estimated costs inflicted on victims is 4.5 times the CJS costs incurred (Schweinhart, 1993, p. 162). However, only 23.3% of the victim costs are tangible (Miller et al., 1996, p. 17). So, the ratio of tangible losses to CJS costs is (4.5)(0.233) = 1.0485.

(l) (Decrease in mother's arrest and jail costs + decrease in child's arrest costs + decrease in CJS costs of child's adult criminal career) * ratio of tangible losses to CJS costs.

CALCULATION OF THE COSTS AND BENEFITS OF THE PERRY PRESCHOOL

In this appendix, we discuss in detail the costs and benefits of the Perry Preschool. (See Chapters Two and Three for more information about the Perry Preschool.) Barnett has published a cost-benefit analysis of the Perry Preschool based on data from the age-27 follow-up (Barnett, 1993). In this analysis, we have used Barnett's results to calculate the savings to government generated from higher employment, reduced welfare usage, reduced criminal justice costs, and reduced special services, which for the Perry Preschool refers to K–12 educational effects.[1] So that the results parallel the Elmira PEIP results, we have converted Barnett's numbers to 1996 dollars and calculated the NPV as of the birth of the participating child, using a 4 percent discount rate.

In Table B.1, the outcomes measured in each of the four categories of savings are listed. Note that not all of the outcomes measured by the Perry Preschool evaluation, nor all of the outcomes measured that could conceivably lead to government savings, are included (see Table 3.2). For example, although the number of teen pregnancies has been measured, and reducing teen pregnancies could lead to government savings, this outcome is not included in this analysis (except to the extent that changes in fertility affect employment and

---

[1] Barnett also includes savings to government from reduced use of adult education and the increased costs to government from greater participation in college; these factors are small and nearly cancel each other out, so we have omitted them.

welfare.)   The average outcomes per participant for both the treatment and control groups are tabulated in Table B.1.

The calculations that lead to the cost and savings numbers in Table 3.6, and the additional monetized benefit numbers in the Perry Preschool column of Table 3.7, are detailed in Table B.2. Program cost is addressed in the first part of Table B.2 (see panel 1). The government savings and additional monetized benefits are addressed in the rest of Table B.2 (see panels 2–13). These are derived from Barnett's estimates of savings and benefits (the dollars have been converted to 1996 dollars using the CPI and discounted), not directly from the outcomes in Table B.1.[2] In each case, the dollar estimate reported is the average savings per participant. Note that in his cost-benefit analysis, Barnett includes an estimate of the monetary value of the intangible losses to crime victims, which we have chosen to omit from our cost-benefit analysis (see Chapter Three).

---

[2]In most cases, Barnett's savings estimates were based on more detailed effects data (e.g., individual education, crime, employment, and welfare histories) rather than on the experimental and control group averages shown in Table B.1. The effects data include one more year of crime data—through age 28.

Table B.1

Program Effects: Perry Preschool

Type of Outcome	Who Is Observed?	Age of Child at Time of Observation	Outcome (Mean)		Treatment Effect (E−C)	Effect Statistically Significant at .05 Level	Source
			Experimental Group	Control Group			
Education effects							
Time in special education through age 19 (% of years)	Child	19	16	28	-12	Yes	(1) p. 26
Years in educably mentally impaired programs through age 27	Child	27	1.1	2.8	-1.7	Yes	(2) p. 62
Years retained in grade through age 27	Child	27	0.5	0.7	-0.2	No	(2) p. 62
High school graduation rate by age 27 (%)	Child	27	66	45	21	Yes	(2) p. 58
Employment effects							
Employment rate at age 19 (%)	Child	19	50	32	18	Yes	(1) p. 47
Employment rate at age 27 (%)	Child	27	71	59	12	No	(2) p. 101
Monthly earnings at age 27 (1993 $)	Child	27	1,219	766	453	Yes	(2) p. 100
Welfare effects							
Received public assistance at age 27 (%)	Child	27	15	32	-17	Yes	(2) p. 107
Received public assistance in last 10 years at age 27 (%)	Child	27	59	80	-21	Yes	(2) p. 107
Crime effects							
Ever arrested by age 27 (%)	Child	27	57	59	-12	Yes	(2) p. 86
Lifetime arrests through age 27	Child	27	2.3	4.6	-2.3	Yes	(2) p. 86

NOTES: Age references are to the age of the focal child. E = experimental; C = control.

SOURCES: (1) Berrueta-Clement et al. (1984). (2) Schweinhart et al. (1993).

Table B.2

Detailed Cost and Benefits: Perry Preschool

Item	Estimate	Year $	NPV at Age	Discount Rate (%)	Source/Comments
1. Cost of Preschool, Child Ages 3 to 4					
Published estimate	$12,356	1992	3	3	Barnett (1993), p. 504
In 1996 $	$13,863	1996	3	3	1996 CPI/1992 CPI = 1.122
NPV at age 0, 4% discount rate	$12,148	1996	0	4	
2. Decrease in Cost to Government of K–12 Education for the Child, Child Ages 5 to 18					
Published estimate	$6,872	1992	3	3	Barnett (1993), p. 504
In 1996 $	$7,710	1996	3	3	1996 CPI/1992 CPI = 1.122
NPV at age 0, 4% discount rate	$6,365	1996	0	4	
3. Increase in Taxes from Increase in Child's Employment Income: Child Ages 19 to 27					
Published estimate	$4,229	1992	3	3	Barnett (1993), p. 504
In 1996 $	$4,745	1996	3	3	1996 CPI/1992 CPI = 1.122
NPV at age 0, 4% discount rate	$3,451	1996	0	4	
4. Increase in Taxes from Increase in Child's Projected Employment Income: Child Ages 28 to 65					
Published estimate	$4,618	1992	3	3	Barnett (1993), p. 504
In 1996 $	$5,181	1996	3	3	1996 CPI/1992 CPI = 1.122
NPV at age 0, 4% discount rate	$3,115	1996	0	4	
5. Decrease in Cost to Government of Welfare Payments to Child, Child Ages 19 to 27					
Published estimate	$2,412	1992	3	3	Barnett (1993), p. 504
In 1996 $	$2,706	1996	3	3	1996 CPI/1992 CPI = 1.122
NPV at age 0, 4% discount rate	$1,968	1996	0	4	

Table B.2—continued

Item	Estimate	Year $	NPV at Age	Discount Rate (%)	Source/Comments
6. Decrease in Cost to Government of Projected Welfare Payments to Child, Child Ages 28 to 65					
Published estimate	$506	1992	3	3	Barnett (1993), p. 504
In 1996 $	$568	1996	3	3	1996 CPI/1992 CPI = 1.122
NPV at age 0, 4% discount rate	$341	1996	0	4	
7. Decrease in CJS Cost of Child's Criminal Activity, Child Ages 15 to 28					
Published estimate	$8,882	1992	3	3	Schweinhart et al. (1993), p. 162
In 1996 $	$9,966	1996	3	3	1996 CPI/1992 CPI = 1.122
NPV at age 0	$7,378	1996	0	4	
8. Decrease in CJS Cost of Child's Projected Criminal Activity, Child Ages 29 to 44					
Published estimate	$3,914	1992	3	3	Schweinhart et al. (1993), p. 162
In 1996 $	$4,392	1996	3	3	1996 CPI/1992 CPI = 1.122
NPV at age 0	$2,817	1996	0	4	
9. Income from Child's Increased Employment, Child Ages 19 to 27					
Published estimate	$10,269	1992	3	3	Barnett (1993), p. 504
In 1996 $	$11,522	1996	3	3	1996 CPI/1992 CPI = 1.122
NPV at age 0	$8,380	1996	0	4	
10. Income from Child's Increased Employment, Child Ages 28 to 65					
Published estimate	$11,215	1992	3	3	Barnett (1993), p. 504
In 1996 $	$12,583	1996	3	3	1996 CPI/1992 CPI = 1.122
NPV at age 0	$7,565	1996	0	4	
11. Decrease in Welfare Payments to Child, Child Ages 19 to 27					
Published estimate	$2,193	1992	3	3	Barnett (1993), p. 504
In 1996 $	$2,461	1996	3	3	1996 CPI/1992 CPI = 1.122
NPV at age 0	$1,790	1996	0	4	

Table B.2—continued

Item	Estimate	Year $	NPV at Age	Discount Rate (%)	Source/Comments
12. Decrease in Projected Welfare Payments to Child, Child Ages 28 to 65					
Published estimate	$460	1992	3	3	Barnett (1993), p. 504
In 1996 $	$516	1996	3	3	1996 CPI/1992 CPI = 1.122
NPV at age 0	$310	1996	0	4	
13. Decrease in Tangible Losses to Crime Victims, Child Ages 15 to 44					
Decrease in CJS costs, child ages 15 to 44	$10,195	1996	0	4	Table B.2, panels 7 and 8
Ratio of tangible losses to CJS costs	1.0485				See Note (a)
Decreased tangible crime losses	$10,690	1996	0	4	

NOTES: NPV = net present value; CPI = Consumer Price Index.

(a) In a typical criminal career, total estimated costs inflicted on victims is 4.5 times the CJS costs incurred (Schweinhart, 1993, p. 162). However, only 23.3 percent of the victim costs are tangible (Miller et al., 1996. p. 17). So the ratio of tangible losses to CJS costs is (4.5)(0.233) = 1.0485.

REFERENCES

Ainsworth, M.D.S., M. Blehar, E. Waters, et al., *Patterns of Attachment*, Hillsdale, N.J.: Lawrence Erlbaum Associates, 1978.

Andrews, S. R., J. B. Bluementhal, D. L. Johnson, et al., "The Skills of Mothering: A Study of Parent-Child Development Centers," *Monographs of the Society for Research in Child Development*, Vol. 47(6), Serial No. 198, 1982.

Aries, Philippe, *Centuries of Childhood: A Social History of Family Life*, New York: Knopf, 1962.

Barnett, W. Steven, "Benefits of Compensatory Preschool Education," *Journal of Human Resources*, Vol. 27(2), Spring 1992, pp. 279–312.

Barnett, W. Steven, "Benefit-Cost Analysis of Preschool Education: Findings from a 25-Year Follow-Up," *American Journal of Orthopsychiatry*, Vol. 63(4), October 1993, pp. 500–508.

Barnett, W. Steven, "Long-Term Effects of Early Childhood Programs on Cognitive and School Outcomes," *The Future of Children*, Vol. 5, Winter 1995, pp. 25–50.

Barnett, W. Steven, and Collette M. Escobar, "Economic Costs and Benefits of Early Intervention," *Handbook of Early Childhood Intervention*, Samuel J. Meisels and Jack P. Shonkoff, eds., New York: Cambridge University Press, 1990, pp. 560–582.

Barnow, B., and G. Cain, "A Reanalysis of the Effect of Head Start on Cognitive Development: Methodology and Empirical Findings," *Journal of Human Resources,* Vol. 12(2), 1977, pp. 177–197.

Benasich, April A., Jeanne Brooks-Gunn, and Beatriz Chu Clewell, "How Do Mothers Benefit from Early Intervention Programs?" *Journal of Applied Developmental Psychology,* Vol. 13, 1992, pp. 311–362.

Bentler, P. M., and J. A. Woodward, "Head-Start Re-Evaluation— Positive Effects Are Not Yet Demonstrable," *Evaluation Quarterly,* Vol. 2(3), 1978, pp. 493–510.

Berrueta-Clement, John R., Lawrence J. Schweinhart, W. Steven Barnett, et al., *Changed Lives: The Effects of the Perry Preschool Program on Youths Through Age 19,* Monographs of the High/Scope Educational Research Foundation, Number Eight, Ypsilanti, Mich.: High/Scope Educational Research Foundation, 1984.

Blair, C., Craig T. Ramey, and J. Michael Hardin, "Early Intervention for Low Birthweight, Premature Infants: Participation and Intellectual Development," *American Journal on Mental Retardation,* Vol. 99(5), 1995, pp. 542–554.

Bloom, Benjamin Samuel, *Stability and Change in Human Characteristics,* New York: John Wiley & Sons, 1964.

Bowlby, J., *Attachment and Loss: Vol. 1. Attachment,* New York: BasicBooks, 1969.

Bradley, R. H., and B. M. Caldwell, "The Relation of Home Environment, Cognitive Competence, and IQ Among Males and Females," *Child Development,* Vol. 51, 1980, pp. 1140–1148.

Bradley, Robert H., Bettye M. Caldwell, Stephen L. Rock, et al., "Home Environment and Cognitive Development in the First 3 Years of Life: A Collaborative Study Involving Six Sites and Three Ethnic Groups in North America," *Developmental Psychology,* Vol. 25(2), 1989, pp. 217–235.

Bronfenbrenner, Urie, *A Report on Longitudinal Programs: Vol. 2. Is Early Intervention Effective?* Washington, D.C.: U.S. Government Printing Office, DHEW Publication Number OHD 74–24, 1974.

Brooks-Gunn, Jeanne, Pamela Klebanov, and Greg J. Duncan, "Ethnic Differences in Children's Intelligence Test Scores: Role of Economic Deprivation, Home Environment, and Maternal Characteristics," *Child Development*, Vol. 67(2), 1996, pp. 396–408.

Brooks-Gunn, Jeanne, Cecelia M. McCarton, Patrick H. Casey, et al., "Early Intervention in Low-Birth-Weight Premature Infants, Results Through Age 5 Years from the Infant Health and Development Program," *Journal of the American Medical Association*, Vol. 272(16), 1994a, pp. 1257–1262.

Brooks-Gunn, Jeanne, Marie C. McCormick, Sam Shapiro, et al., "The Effects of Early Education Intervention on Maternal Employment, Public Assistance, and Health Insurance: The Infant Health and Development Program," *American Journal of Public Health*, Vol. 84(6), 1994b, pp. 924–931.

Burlingham, Dorothy, and Anna Freud, *Enfants sans famille (Children without Families)*, Paris: Presses Universitaires de France, 1949a.

Burlingham, Dorothy, and Anna Freud, *Kriegskinder (War Children)*, London: Imago, 1949b.

Burlingham, Dorothy, and Anna Freud, *Anstaltskinder; Argumente fuer und gegen die Anstaltserziehung von Kleinkindern (Children in Institutions; Arguments for and Against the Education of Small Children in Institutions)*, London: Imago, 1950.

Campbell, Frances A., and Craig T. Ramey, "Effects of Early Intervention on Intellectual and Academic Achievement: A Follow-Up Study of Children from Low-Income Families," *Child Development*, Vol. 65(2, Spec. No.), 1994, pp. 684–689.

Campbell, Frances A., and Craig T. Ramey, "Cognitive and School Outcomes for High-Risk African American Students at Middle Adolescence: Positive Effects of Early Intervention," *American Education Research Journal*, Vol. 32(4), 1995, pp. 743–772.

Carey, S., and Rochel Gelman, eds., *The Epigenesis of Mind: Essays on Biology and Cognition*, Hillsdale, N.J.: Lawrence Erlbaum Associates, 1991.

Carlson, V., D. Cicchetti, D. Barnett, et al., "Disorganized/Disoriented Attachment Relationships in Maltreated Infants," *Developmental Psychology*, Vol. 25(4), 1989, pp. 525–531.

Carnegie Corporation of New York, *Starting Points, Meeting the Needs of Our Youngest Children*, 1994.

Carnegie Corporation of New York, *Years of Promise, a Comprehensive Learning Strategy for America's Children*, 1996.

Centers for Disease Control, U.S. Department of Health and Human Services, "Measles—United States 1989 and First 20 Weeks, 1990," *Morbidity and Mortality Weekly Report*, Vol. 39(21), pp. 353–363.

Cicirelli, Victor G., *The Impact of Head Start: An Evaluation of the Effects of Head Start on Children's Cognitive and Affective Development*, Athens, Ohio, and New York: Ohio University, and Westinghouse Learning Corporation, 1969.

Clarke-Stewart, K. Alison, "A Home Is Not a School: The Effects of Child Care on Children's Development," *Journal of Social Issues*, Vol. 47(2), 1991, pp. 105–123.

Cohen, A. J., "A Brief History of Federal Financing for Child Care in the United States," *Financing Child Care*, 1996, pp. 26–40.

Cohen, S., and Leila Beckwith, "Preterm Infant Interaction with the Caregiver in the First Year of Life and Competence at Age Two," *Child Development*, Vol. 50, 1979, pp. 767–776.

Coleman, James S., et al., *Equality of Educational Opportunity*, Washington, D.C.: U.S. Department of Health, Education, and Welfare, 1966.

Congressional Budget Office (CBO), Congress of the Unites States, *Reducing the Deficit: Spending and Revenue Options*, Washington, D.C.: U.S. Government Printing Office, 1997.

Copple, Carol E., Marvin G. Cline, and Allen N. Smith, *Path to the Future: Long-Term Effects of Head Start in the Philadelphia School District*, Washington, D.C.: U.S. Department of Health and Human Services, PS 017031, 1987.

Cowan, W. M., "The Development of the Brain," *Scientific American*, Vol. 241(3), September 1979, pp. 113–133.

Cravens, Hamilton, *Before Head Start: The Iowa Station and America's Children*, Chapel Hill: The University of North Carolina Press, 1993.

Currie, Janet M., *Welfare and the Well-Being of Children*, Chur, Switzerland: Harwood Academic, Fundamentals of Pure and Applied Economics Series, 1995.

Currie, Janet M., and Duncan Thomas, "Does Head Start Make a Difference?" *The American Economic Review*, Vol. 85(3), 1995, pp. 341–364.

Deutsch, Martin, *The Disadvantaged Child; Selected Papers of Martin Deutsch and Associates*, New York: BasicBooks, 1967.

Duncan, Greg J., and Jeanne Brooks-Gunn, eds., *Consequences of Growing up Poor*, New York: Russell Sage Foundation, 1997.

Epstein, H., "Correlated Brain and Intelligence Development in Humans," *Development and Evolution of Brain Size*, Martin E. Hahn, Craig Jensen, and Bruce C. Dudek, eds., New York: Academic Press, 1979.

Erickson, Erik Homburger, *The Life Cycle Completed: A Review*, New York, W. W. Norton & Co., 1985.

Flanagan, D. P., Judy L. Genshaft, and Patti L. Harrison, eds., *Contemporary Intellectual Assessment: Theories, Tests, and Issues*, New York: Guilford Press, 1997.

General Accounting Office (GAO), *Head Start: Research Provides Little Information on Impact of Current Program*, GAO/HEHS-97-59, Washington, D.C.: U.S. Government Printing Office, April 1997.

Gesell, Arnold Lucius, and Helen Thompson, *Infant Behavior: Its Genesis and Growth*, New York: McGraw-Hill, 1934.

Gomby, D. S., M. B. Larner, C. S. Stevenson, et al., "Long-Term Outcomes of Early Childhood Programs: Analysis and Recommendations," *The Future of Children*, Vol. 5, Winter 1995, pp. 6–24.

Gray, S. W., and R. A. Klaus, "The Early Training Project: A Seventh Year Report," *Child Development*, Vol. 41(4), 1970, pp. 909–924.

Gray, S. W., and Barbara K. Ramsey, "The Early Training Project: A Life-Span View," *Human Development*, Vol. 25(1), 1982, pp. 48–57.

Gray, S. W., Barbara K. Ramsey, and R. A. Klaus, *From 3 to 20: The Early Training Project*, Baltimore, Md.: University Park Press, 1982.

Greenwood, Peter W., Karyn E. Model, C. Peter Rydell, and James Chiesa, *Diverting Children from a Life of Crime: Measuring Costs and Benefits*, Santa Monica, Calif.: RAND, MR-699-UCB/RC/F, 1996.

Greenwood, Peter W., C. Peter Rydell, Allan F. Abrahamse, Jonathan P. Caulkins, James Chiesa, Karyn E. Model, and Stephen P. Klein, *Three Strikes and You're Out: Estimated Benefits and Costs of California's New Mandatory-Sentencing Law*, Santa Monica, Calif.: RAND, MR-509-RC, 1994.

Grubb, W. Norton, *Evaluating Job Training Programs in the United States: Evidence and Explanations*, National Center for Research in Vocational Education, Technical Report, May 1995.

Gueron, Judith M., Edward Pauly, and Cameron M. Lougy, *From Welfare to Work*, New York: Russell Sage Foundation, 1991.

Guralnick, Michael J., ed., *Effectiveness of Early Intervention*, Baltimore, Md.: Paul Brookes Publishing, 1997.

Haggerty, R. J., "The Changing Role of the Pediatrician in Child Health Care," *American Journal of Diseases of Children*, Vol. 127, 1984, pp. 545–549.

Haveman, R., and B. Wolfe, "The Determinants of Children's Attainments: A Review of Methods and Findings," *Journal of Economic Literature*, Vol. 33, December 1995, pp. 1829–1878.

Hay, Joel W., and Robert S. Daum, "Cost-Benefit Analysis of Haemophilus Influenzae Type B Prevention: Conjugate Vaccination at Eighteen Months of Age," *Pediatric Infectious Diseases Journal*, Vol. 9(4), 1990, pp. 246–252.

Hebb, Donald Olding, *The Organization of Behavior: A Neuropsychological Theory*, New York: John Wiley & Sons, 1949.

Hinman, A. R., and J. P. Koplan, "Pertussis and Pertussis Vaccine: Further Analysis of Benefits, Risks and Costs," *Developmental Biology Standard*, Vol. 61, 1984, pp. 429–437.

Honig, A. S., and J. Ronald Lally, "The Family Development Research Program: Retrospective Review," *Early Child Development and Care*, Vol. 10, 1982, pp. 41–62.

Hosek, James R., and Robert E. Levine, eds., *The New Fiscal Federalism and the Social Safety Net: A View From California*, Santa Monica, Calif.: RAND, CF-123-RC, 1996.

Hunt, Joseph McVicker, *Intelligence and Experience*, New York: John Wiley & Sons, 1961.

Hutchins, V. L., "Maternal and Child Health Bureau: Roots," *Pediatrics*, Vol. 94(5), 1994, pp. 695–699.

Infant Health and Development Project (IHDP), "Enhancing the Outcomes of Low-Birth-Weight Premature Infants," *Journal of the American Medical Association*, Vol. 263(22), 1990, pp. 3035–3042.

Institute for Research on Poverty (IRP), "Do Intervention Programs for Young Children Reduce Delinquency and Crime?" *Focus*, Vol. 19(1), Summer/Fall 1997a.

Institute for Research on Poverty (IRP), "Two-Generation Programs: A Roadmap to National Evaluations," *Focus*, Vol. 19(1), Summer/Fall 1997b.

Jensen, A. R., "How Much Can We Boost IQ and Scholastic Achievement?" *Harvard Educational Review*, Vol. 39(1), 1969, pp. 1–123.

Johnson, Dale L., and James N. Breckenridge, "The Houston Parent-Child Development Center and the Primary Prevention of Behavior Problems in Young Children," *American Journal of Community Psychology*, Vol. 10(3), 1982, pp. 305–316.

Johnson, Dale L., et al., "The Houston Parent-Child Development Center: A Parent Education Program for Mexican-American

Families," *American Journal of Orthopsychiatry*, Vol. 44(1), 1974, pp. 121–128.

Johnson, Dale L., and Todd Walker, "A Follow-Up Evaluation of the Houston Parent-Child Development Center: School Performance," *Journal of Early Intervention*, Vol. 15(3), 1991, pp. 226–236.

Kitzman, Harriet, David L. Olds, Charles R. Henderson, et al., "Effect of Prenatal and Infancy Home Visitation by Nurses on Pregnancy Outcomes, Childhood Injuries, and Repeated Childbearing: A Randomized Controlled Trial," *Journal of the American Medical Association*, Vol. 278(8), 1997, pp. 644–652.

Klerman, Lorraine V., *Alive and Well? A Research and Policy Review of Health Programs for Poor Young Children*, New York: National Center for Children in Poverty, Columbia University School of Public Health, 1991.

Lalonde, Robert J., "The Promise of Public Sector–Sponsored Training Programs," *Journal of Economic Perspectives*, Vol. 9(2), Spring 1995.

Lally, J. Ronald, Peter L. Mangione, and Alice S. Honig, "The Syracuse University Family Development Research Program: Long-Range Impact of an Early Intervention with Low-Income Children and Their Families," *Parent Education as Early Childhood Intervention: Emerging Directions in Theory, Research and Practice*, D. R. Powell and I. E. Sigel, eds., Norwood, N.J.: Ablex Publishing Corporation, 1988.

Lazar, Irving, and Richard Darlington, "Lasting Effects of Early Education: A Report from the Consortium for Longitudinal Studies," *Monographs of the Society for Research in Child Development*, Vol. 47(2–4), Serial No. 195, 1982.

Liaw, Fong-ruey, and Jeanne Brooks-Gunn, "Cumulative Familial Risks and Low-Birthweight Children's Cognitive and Behavioral Development," *Journal of Clinical Child Psychology*, Vol. 23(4), 1994, pp. 360–372.

Lubeck, Sally, "Children and Families 'At Promise,'" *Children and Families "At Promise": Deconstructing the Discourse of Risk*, B. B.

Swadener and S. Lubeck, eds., Albany, N.Y.: State University of New York Press, 1995.

Lyons-Ruth, K., L. Alpern, and B. Repacholi, "Disorganized Attachment Classification and Maternal Psychosocial Problems as Predictors of Hostile-Aggressive Behavior in the Preschool Classroom," *Child Development*, Vol. 64, 1993, pp. 572–585.

Magidson, Jay, and Dag Soerbom, "Adjusting for the Confounding Factors in Quasi-Experiments: Another Reanalysis of the Westinghouse Head Start Evaluation," *Educational Evaluation and Policy Analysis*, Vol. 4(3), 1982, pp. 321–329.

Martin, Sandra L., Craig T. Ramey, and Sharon Ramey, "The Prevention of Intellectual Impairment in Children of Impoverished Families: Findings of a Randomized Trial of Educational Day Care," *American Journal of Public Health*, Vol. 80(7), 1990, pp. 844–847.

Mathematica Policy Research, *The Savings in Medicaid Costs for Newborns and Their Mothers from Prenatal Participation in the WIC Program*, Washington, D.C.: U.S. Department of Agriculture, 1990.

McCarton, Cecelia M., Jeanne Brooks-Gunn, Ina F. Wallace, et al., "Results at Age 8 Years of Early Intervention for Low-Birth-Weight Premature Infants, The Infant Health and Development Program," *Journal of the American Medical Association*, Vol. 277(2), 1997, pp. 126–132.

McCormick, Marie C., Jeanne Brooks-Gunn, S. Shapiro, April A. Benasich, G. Black, R. T. Gross, "Health Care Use Among Young Children in Day Care: Results in a Randomized Trial of Early Intervention, *Journal of the American Medical Association*, Vol. 265, 1991, pp. 2212–2217.

McCormick, Marie C., Cecelia M. McCarton, C. Tonascia, and Jeanne Brooks-Gunn, "Early Educational Intervention for Very Low Birth Weight Infants: Results from the Infant Health and Development Program, *Journal of Pediatrics*, Vol. 123, 1993, pp. 527–533.

McGill, Dagmar E., Sharon F. Mihalic, and Jennifer K. Grotpeter, *Blueprints for Violence Prevention: Big Brothers Big Sisters of*

America, Book Two, Delbert S. Elliott, series ed., Boulder Colo.: Institute of Behavioral Sciences, Regents of the University of Colorado, 1997.

McKey, Ruth Hubbell, Larry Condelli, Harriet Ganson, et al., *The Impact of Head Start on Children, Families and Communities, Final Report of the Head Start Evaluation, Synthesis and Utilization Project*, Washington, D.C.: U.S. Department of Health and Human Services, 85-31193, 1985.

Meisels, Samuel J., and Jack P. Shonkoff, eds., *Handbook of Early Childhood Intervention*, New York: Cambridge University Press, 1990.

Melton, G. B., and S. Megan, "The Concept of Entitlement and Its Incompatibility with American Legal Culture," *Visions of Entitlement: The Care and Education of America's Children*, Mary A. Jensen and Stacie G. Goffin, eds., Albany, N.Y.: State University of New York Press, 1993.

Miller, Ted R., Mark A. Cohen, and Brian Wiersema, *Victim Costs and Consequences: A New Look*, Washington, D.C.: National Institute of Justice, 1996.

Nash, J. Madeleine, "Fertile Minds," *Time*, Vol. 149(5), Feb. 3, 1997, pp. 48–56.

National Governors' Association (NGA), *Promising Practices to Improve Results for Young Children*, Washington, D.C.: NGA, 1997.

National Science and Technology Council, Committee on Fundamental Science, and the Committee on Health, Safety, and Food, *Investing in Our Future: A National Research Initiative for America's Children for the 21st Century*, Washington, D.C.: Executive Office of the President, Office of Science and Technology Policy, April 1997.

Nightingale, Demetra S., and Robert H. Haveman, eds., *The Work Alternative: Welfare Reform and the Realities of the Job Market*, Washington, D.C.: Urban Institute Press, 1995.

Olds, David L., *Reducing Risks for Childhood-Onset Conduct Disorder with Prenatal and Early Childhood Home Visitation*, paper presented at the American Public Health Association Pre-Conference Workshop: Prevention Science and Families: Mental Health Research and Public Health Policy Implications, New York, November 16, 1996.

Olds, David L., and A. M. Cooper, "Dialogue with Other Sciences: Opportunities for Mutual Gain [editorial]," *International Journal of Psycho-Analysis*, Vol. 78(2), 1997.

Olds, David L., John Eckenrode, Charles R. Henderson, Jr., et al., "Long-Term Effects of Home Visitation on Maternal Life Course, Child Abuse and Neglect, and Children's Arrests: Fifteen Year Follow-Up of a Randomized Trial," *Journal of the American Medical Association*, Vol. 278(8), 1997, pp. 637–643.

Olds, David L., Charles R. Henderson, Jr., and Harriet Kitzman, "Does Prenatal and Infancy Nurse Home Visitation Have Enduring Effects on Qualities of Parental Caregiving and Child Health at 25 to 50 Months of Life?" *Pediatrics*, Vol. 93(1), 1994, pp. 89–98.

Olds, David L., Charles R. Henderson, Jr., Charles Phelps, Harriet Kitzman, and Carole Hanks, "Effect of Prenatal and Infancy Nurse Home Visitation on Government Spending," *Medical Care*, Vol. 31(2), February 1993, pp. 155–174.

Olds, David L., Charles R. Henderson, Jr., Robert Tatelbaum, Robert Chamberlin, et al., "Improving the Delivery of Prenatal Care and Outcomes of Pregnancy: A Randomized Trial of Nurse Home Visitation," *Pediatrics*, Vol. 77(1), 1986a, pp. 16–28.

Olds, David L., Charles R. Henderson, Jr., Robert Tatelbaum, Robert Chamberlin, et al., "Preventing Child Abuse and Neglect: A Randomized Trial of Nurse Home Visitation," *Pediatrics*, Vol. 78(1), 1986b, pp. 65–78.

Olds, David L., Charles R. Henderson, Jr., Robert Tatelbaum, et al., "Improving the Life-Course Development of Socially Disadvantaged Mothers: A Randomized Trial of Nurse Home Visitation," *American Journal of Public Health*, Vol. 78(11), 1988, pp. 1436–1445.

Olds, David L., and Harriet Kitzman, "Review of Research on Home Visiting for Pregnant Women and Parents of Young Children," *The Future of Children*, Vol. 3, Winter 1993, pp. 53–92.

Parker, S., S. Greer, and B. Zuckerman, "Double Jeopardy," *Pediatric Clinics of North America*, Vol. 35, 1988, pp. 1227–1240.

Parmelee, A. H., Jr., *The History of Pediatrics and Well-Child Care, 1888–1940*, Los Angeles, Calif.: UCLA Department of Pediatrics Grand Rounds, 1994.

Pentz, Mary Ann, Sharon F. Mihalic, and Jennifer K. Grotpeter, *Blueprints for Violence Prevention: The Midwestern Prevention Project*, Book One, Delbert S. Elliott, series ed., Boulder Colo.: Institute of Behavioral Sciences, Regents of the University of Colorado, 1997.

Phillips, D. A., K. McCartney, and S. Scarr, "Child-Care Quality and Children's Social Development," *Developmental Psychology*, Vol. 23, 1987, pp. 537–543.

Piaget, Jean, *La Psychologie de l'Intelligence (The Psychology of Intelligence)*, Paris: Armand Colin, 1947.

Piaget, Jean, and Barbel Inhelder, "Diagnosis of Mental Operations and Theory of the Intelligence," *American Journal of Mental Deficiency*, Vol. 51, 1947, pp. 401–406.

Pollitt, E., "Iron Deficiency and Educational Deficiency," *Nutrition Reviews*, Vol. 55(4), 1997, pp. 133–141.

Purves, Dale, *Neural Activity and the Growth of the Brain (Lezioni Lincee)*, New York: Cambridge University Press, 1994.

Ramey, Craig T., Donna M. Bryant, Joseph J. Sparling, et al., "Project CARE: A Comparison of Two Early Intervention Strategies to Prevent Retarded Development," *Topics in Early Childhood Special Education*, Vol. 5(2), 1985, pp. 12–25.

Ramey, Craig T., Donna M. Bryant, Barbara H. Wasik, et al., "Infant Health and Development Program for Low Birth Weight, Premature Infants: Program Elements, Family Participation, and Child Intelligence," *Pediatrics*, Vol. 3, March 1992, pp. 454–465.

Ramey, Craig T., and Frances A. Campbell, "Educational Intervention for Children at Risk for Mild Mental Retardation: A Longitudinal Analysis," *Frontiers of Knowledge in Mental Retardation (Vol. I)*, P. Miller, ed., Baltimore, Md.: Baltimore University Park Press, 1981.

Ramey, Craig T., Bruce Dorval, and Lynne Baker-Ward, "Group Day Care and Socially Disadvantaged Families: Effects on the Child and the Family," *Advances in Early Education and Day Care*, Vol. 3, 1983, pp. 69–106.

Ramey, Craig T., and S. L. Ramey, "Which Children Benefit the Most from Early Intervention?" *Pediatrics*, Vol. 6(2), Dec. 1994, pp. 1064–1066.

Reville, Robert T., and Jacob Alex Klerman, "Job Training: The Impact on California of Further Consolidation and Devolution," *The New Fiscal Federalism and the Social Safety Net: A View from California*, James Hosek and Robert Levine, eds., Santa Monica, Calif.: RAND, CF-123-RC, 1996.

Reynolds, Arthur J., *The Chicago Child-Parent Centers: A Longitudinal Study of Extended Early Childhood Intervention*, Discussion Paper No. 1126-97, Madison, Wisc.: Institute for Research on Poverty, 1997 (also available on the Web: http://www.ssc.wisc.edu/irp/).

Reynolds, Arthur J., "Effects of a Preschool Plus Follow-On Intervention for Children at Risk," *Developmental Psychology*, Vol. 30(6), 1994, pp. 787–804.

Reynolds, Arthur J., H. Chang, and Judy A. Temple, *Early Educational Intervention and Juvenile Delinquency: Findings from the Chicago Longitudinal Study*, paper presented at the SRCD Seminar on Early Intervention Effects on Delinquency and Crime, Washington, D.C., April 1997.

Reynolds, Arthur J., Emily Mann, Wendy Miedel, and Paul Smokowski, "The State of Early Childhood Intervention: Effectiveness, Myths and Realities, New Directions," *Focus*, Vol. 19(1), Summer/Fall 1997.

Reynolds, Arthur J., and Judy A. Temple, "Quasi-Experimental Estimates of the Effects of a Preschool Intervention," *Evaluation Review*, Vol. 19(4), 1995, pp. 347–373.

Richmond, Arthur J., and Catherine C. Ayoub, "Evolution of Early Intervention Philosophy," *Implementing Early Intervention: From Research to Effective Practice*, Donna M. Bryant and Mimi A. Graham, eds., New York: The Guilford Press, 1993.

Rossi, P. H., and Howard E. Freeman, *Evaluation: A Systematic Approach*, Thousand Oaks, Calif.: Sage, 1993.

Roupp, Richard, Jeffrey Travers, Frederic Glantz, et al., *Children at the Center: Summary Findings and Their Implications*, Cambridge, Mass.: Abt Associates, 1979.

Sameroff, A. J., and M. J. Chandler, "Reproductive Risk and the Continuum of Caretaking Casualty," *Review of Child Development Research*, F. D. Horowitz, ed., Chicago: University of Chicago Press, 1975.

Sander, Louis W., "A 25-Year Follow-Up: Some Reflections on Personality Development Over the Long Term. Special Issue: Papers from the Third Congress of the World Association for Infant Psychiatry and Allied Disciplines," *Infant Mental Health Journal*, Vol. 8(3), 1987, pp. 210–220.

Schore, Allan N., *Affect Regulation and the Origin of the Self: The Neurobiology of Emotional Development*, Hillsdale, N.J.: Lawrence Erlbaum Associates, 1994.

Schwartz, J., "Low-Level Lead Exposure and Children's IQ: A Meta-Analysis and Search for a Threshold," *Environmental Research*, Vol. 65(1), 1994, pp. 42–55.

Schweinhart, Lawrence J., Helen V. Barnes, and David P. Weikart, with W. Steven Barnett and Ann S. Epstein, *Significant Benefits: The High/Scope Perry Preschool Study Through Age 27*, Monographs of the High/Scope Educational Research Foundation, Number Ten, Ypsilanti, Mich.: High/Scope Educational Research Foundation, 1993.

Schweinhart, Lawrence J., and David P. Weikart, *Young Children Grow Up: The Effects of the Perry Preschool Program on Youths Through Age 15*, Monographs of the High/Scope Educational Research Foundation, Number Seven, Ypsilanti, Mich.: High/Scope Educational Research Foundation, 1980.

Seitz, Victoria, "Intervention Programs for Impoverished Children: A Comparison of Educational and Family Support Models," *Annals of Child Development*, Vol. 7, 1990, pp. 73–103.

Shadish, W. R. J., Thomas D. Cook, and Laura C. Leviton, *Foundations of Program Evaluation: Theories of Practice*, Thousand Oaks, Calif.: Sage, 1995.

Solso, Robert L., ed., *Mind and Brain Sciences in the 21st Century*, Cambridge, Mass.: MIT Press, 1997.

Spiker, D., Joan Ferguson, and Jeanne Brooks-Gunn, "Enhancing Maternal Interactive Behavior and Child Social Competence in Low Birth Weight, Premature Infants," *Child Development*, Vol. 64, 1993, pp. 754–768.

Spitz, R. A., *The First Year of Life: A Psychoanalytic Study of Normal and Deviant Development of Object Relations*, New York: International Universities Press, 1965.

Sprigle, J. E., and L. Schaefer, "Longitudinal Evaluation of the Effects of Two Compensatory Preschool Programs on Fourth- Through Sixth-Grade Students," *Developmental Psychology*, Vol. 21(2), 1985, pp. 702–708.

St. Pierre, R. G., Jean I. Layzer, and H. V. Barnes, "Two-Generation Programs: Design, Cost, and Short-Term Effectiveness," *The Future of Children*, Vol. 5, Winter 1995, pp. 76–93.

Studer, Marlena, "Nonparental Child Care Environments: Differences in Preschool Cognitive Skills by Type of Care," *Sociological Studies of Child Development*, Vol. 5, 1992a, pp. 23–47.

Studer, Marlena, "Quality of Center Care and Preschool Cognitive Outcomes: Differences by Family Income," *Sociological Studies of Child Development*, Vol. 5, 1992b, pp. 49–72.

Swadener, Beth Blue, and Sally Lubeck, "The Social Construction of Children and Families 'At Risk,'" *Children and Families "At Promise": Deconstructing the Discourse of Risk*, Beth Blue Swadener and Sally Lubeck, eds., Albany, N.Y.: State University of New York Press, 1995.

U.S. Bureau of the Census, *Statistical Abstract of the United States: 1996* (114th edition), Washington, D.C., 1996.

U.S. Department of Labor, *What's Working (and What's Not): A Summary of Research on the Economic Impacts of Employment and Training Programs*, Washington, D.C.: Office of the Chief Economist, U.S. Department of Labor, January 1995.

Wasik, Barbara Hanna, Craig T. Ramey, Donna M. Bryant, et al., "A Longitudinal Study of Two Early Intervention Strategies: Project CARE," *Child Development*, Vol. 61, 1990, pp. 1682–1696.

Watson, John B., "Psychology As the Behaviourist Views It," *Psychological Review*, Vol. 20(2), 1913, pp. 158–177.

Weikart, David P., J. T. Bond, and J. T. McNeil, *The Ypsilanti Perry Preschool Project: Preschool Years and Longitudinal Results Through Fourth Grade*, Monographs of the High/Scope Educational Research Foundation, Number Three, Ypsilanti, Mich.: High/Scope Educational Research Foundation, 1978.

Weiss, C. H., *Evaluation Action Programs: Readings in Social Action and Education*. Boston: Allyn and Bacon, 1972.

Weiss, C. H., "Where Politics and Evaluation Research Meet," *Evaluation*, Vol. 1, 1973, pp. 37–45.

Whitebook, Marcy, Carole Howes, Deborah Phillips, et al., *The National Child Care Staffing Study*, Oakland, Calif.: Child Care Employee Project, 1989.

Wolff, Max, and Annie Stein, *Study I: Six Months Later, A Comparison of Children Who Had Head Start, Summer 1965, with Their Classmates in Kindergarten*, Washington, D.C.: Research and Evaluation Office, Project Head Start, Office of Economic Opportunity, 1966.

Yoshikawa, H., "Long-Term Effects of Early Childhood Programs on Social Outcomes and Delinquency," *The Future of Children*, Vol. 5, Winter 1995, pp. 51–75.

Zaslow, M., "Variation in Child Care Quality and Its Implications for Children," *Journal of Social Issues*, Vol. 47(2), 1991, pp. 125–139.

Zeanah, Charles H., ed., *Handbook of Infant Mental Health*, New York: The Guilford Press, 1993.

Zigler, Edward F., "Foreword," *Handbook of Early Childhood Intervention*, Samuel J. Meisels and Jack P. Shonkoff, eds., New York: Cambridge University Press, 1990.

Zigler, Edward F., Sharon L. Kagan, and Nancy W. Hall, eds., *Children, Families, and Government: Preparing for the Twenty-First Century*, New York: Cambridge University Press, 1996.

Zigler, Edward F., and Susan Muenchow, *Head Start: The Inside Story of America's Most Successful Educational Experiment*, New York: BasicBooks, 1992.

Zigler, Edward F., and Sally J. Styfco, *Head Start and Beyond: A National Plan for Extended Childhood Intervention*, New Haven, Conn.: Yale University Press, 1993.